HENRY FOSS

Biography Today

Profiles of People of Interest to Young Readers

Scientists & Inventors Series

Volume 4

Laurie Lanzen Harris
Executive Editor

Cherie D. Abbey
Co-Editor

FEB   2001

615 Griswold Street • Detroit, Michigan 48226

Laurie Lanzen Harris, *Executive Editor*
Cherie D. Abbey, *Co-Editor*
Kevin Hillstrom and Laurie Hillstrom, *Sketch Writers*
Joan Margeson and Barry Puckett, *Research Associates*

Omnigraphics, Inc.

* * *

Peter E. Ruffner, *Senior Vice President*
Matthew P. Barbour, *Vice President — Operations*
Laurie Lanzen Harris, *Vice President — Editorial*
Thomas J. Murphy, *Vice President — Finance*
Jane J. Steele, *Marketing Coordinator*
Kevin Hayes, *Production Coordinator*

* * *

Frederick G. Ruffner, Jr., Publisher

This book is printed on acid-free paper meeting the ANSI Z39.48 Standard.
The infinity symbol that appears above indicates that the paper in this book
meets that standard.

Printed in the United States

Contents

Preface

Welcome to the fourth volume of the **Biography Today Scientists and Inventors Series**. We are publishing this series in response to the growing number of suggestions from our readers, who want more coverage of more people in *Biography Today*. Several volumes, covering **Artists, Authors, Scientists and Inventors, Sports Figures, and World Leaders**, have appeared thus far in the Subject Series. Each of these hardcover volumes is 200 pages in length and covers approximately 12 individuals of interest to readers ages 9 and above. The length and format of the entries will be like those found in the regular issues of *Biography Today*, but there is **no duplication** between the regular series and the special subject volumes.

The Plan of the Work

As with the regular issues of *Biography Today*, this special subject volume on **Scientists and Inventors** was especially created to appeal to young readers in a format they can enjoy reading and readily understand. Each volume contains alphabetically arranged sketches. Each entry provides at least one picture of the individual profiled, and bold-faced rubrics lead the reader to information on birth, youth, early memories, education, first jobs, marriage and family, career highlights, memorable experiences, hobbies, and honors and awards. Each of the entries ends with a list of easily accessible sources designed to lead the student to further reading on the individual and a current address. Obituary entries are also included, written to provide a perspective on the individual's entire career. Obituaries are clearly marked in both the table of contents and at the beginning of the entry.

Biographies are prepared by Omnigraphics editors after extensive research, utilizing the most current materials available. Those sources that are generally available to students appear in the list of further reading at the end of the sketch.

Indexes

A new index now appears in all *Biography Today* publications. In an effort to make the index easier to use, we have combined the **Name** and **General Index** into one, called the **General Index**. This new index contains the names of all individuals who have appeared in *Biography Today* since the series began. The names appear in bold faced type, followed by the issue in which they appeared. The General Index also contains the occupations and ethnic and minority origins of individuals profiled. The General Index is cumulative, including references to all individuals who have appeared in the *Biography Today* General Series and the *Biography Today* Special Subject volumes since the series began in 1992.

The Birthday Index and Places of Birth Index will continue to appear in all Special Subject volumes.

Our Advisors

This volume was reviewed by an Advisory Board comprised of librarians, children's literature specialists, and reading instructors so that we could make sure that the concept of this publication — to provide a readable and accessible biographical magazine for young readers — was on target. They evaluated the title as it developed, and their suggestions have proved invaluable. Any errors, however, are ours alone. We'd like to list the Advisory Board members, and to thank them for their efforts.

Sandra Arden, *Retired*
Assistant Director
Troy Public Library, Troy, MI

Gail Beaver
Ann Arbor Huron High School Library
and the University of Michigan School
of Information and Library Studies
Ann Arbor, MI

Marilyn Bethel
Pompano Beach Branch Library
Pompano Beach, FL

Eileen Butterfield
Waterford Public Library
Waterford, CT

Linda Carpino
Detroit Public Library
Detroit, MI

Helen Gregory
Grosse Pointe Public Library
Grosse Pointe, MI

Jane Klasing, *Retired*
School Board of Broward County
Fort Lauderdale, FL

Marlene Lee
Broward County Public Library System
Fort Lauderdale, FL

Judy Liskov
Waterford Public Library
Waterford, CT

Sylvia Mavrogenes
Miami-Dade Public Library System
Miami, FL

Carole J. McCollough
Wayne State University School of
Library Science, Detroit, MI

Deborah Rutter
Russell Library, Middletown, CT

Barbara Sawyer
Groton Public Library and Information
Center, Groton, CT

Renee Schwartz
School Board of Broward County
Fort Lauderdale, FL

Lee Sprince
Broward West Regional Library
Fort Lauderdale, FL

Susan Stewart, *Retired*
Birney Middle School Reading
Laboratory, Southfield, MI

Ethel Stoloff, *Retired*
Birney Middle School Library
Southfield, MI

Our Advisory Board stressed to us that we should not shy away from controversial or unconventional people in our profiles, and we have tried to follow their advice. The Advisory Board also mentioned that the sketches might be useful in reluctant reader and adult literacy programs, and we would value any comments librarians might have about the suitability of our magazine for those purposes.

Your Comments Are Welcome

Our goal is to be accurate and up-to-date, to give young readers information they can learn from and enjoy. Now we want to know what you think. Take a look at this issue of *Biography Today*, on approval. Write or call me with your comments. We want to provide an excellent source of biographical information for young people. Let us know how you think we're doing.

> Laurie Harris
> Executive Editor, *Biography Today*
> Omnigraphics, Inc.
> 615 Griswold Street
> Detroit, MI 48226
> Fax: 1-800-875-1340

David Attenborough 1926-

English Naturalist, Documentary Filmmaker, and Writer
Creator of Such Works as *Life on Earth, The Living Planet,* and *The Life of Birds*

BIRTH

David Frederick Attenborough was born in London, England, on May 8, 1926. His parents were Frederick Levi Attenborough, a professor and administrator at University College in Leicester, England, and Mary (Clegg) Attenborough, a schoolteacher. David was the second of three sons born to the Attenboroughs. His older brother, Richard, grew up to become a well-known actor and film director. His younger brother, John, became a successful automobile industry executive.

"[My father] was a marvelous educator, a great teacher, and he believed that the way you teach children is to allow them to discover for themselves. From the age of six, I was always roaming the countryside in search of fossils or wild animals. I'd find a fossil and show it to my father and he'd say, 'Good, good, tell me all about it.' So I responded and became my own expert. After a while I got a tank of tropical fish, and then I'd explain to him how they bred."

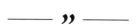

YOUTH

Attenborough was introduced to the wonders of science and the natural world at a young age. Distinguished scientists and biologists frequently visited his childhood home to see his parents, and their discussions of various scientific issues made a big impression on him. "They were my gods," Attenborough recalled, referring to the scholars and scientists who passed through his early life. Their example helped him realize at an early age that knowledge was "what made you admirable [and] what made adults important," he said.

Naturally curious, Attenborough spent countless hours of his youth exploring the hills and woods around his Leicester home or reading about the many animals that fascinated him. Both of his parents encouraged him in these activities, but his father was particularly effective in giving his second son a life-long interest in science. "[My father] was a marvelous educator, a great teacher, and he believed that the way you teach children is to allow them to discover for themselves," remembered Attenborough. "From the age of six, I was always roaming the countryside in search of fossils or wild animals. I'd find a fossil and show it to my father and he'd say, 'Good, good, tell me all about it.' So I responded and became my own expert. After a while I got a tank of tropical fish, and then I'd explain to him how they bred."

EDUCATION

Attenborough attended Wyggeston Grammar School for Boys in Leicester, where he earned good grades. After graduating, he enrolled in Clare

College in Cambridge, England. When Attenborough first started at Clare, he intended to earn a degree in geology, the study of the origins and structure of the earth. He realized after a few semesters, though, that he was more interested in learning about the many creatures that live around the world. As a result, he switched his emphasis of study to zoology, the biological study of animals. He graduated from Clare with a master's degree in zoology in 1947. This marked the end of his formal schooling, except for several graduate courses that he took at London University in the early 1960s in anthropology (the study of the origins and development of mankind).

CAREER HIGHLIGHTS

Finding His Place in the World

After leaving Clare in 1947, Attenborough spent about a year in England's Royal Navy, where he rose to the rank of lieutenant. In 1949 he left the military and accepted a position as an editorial assistant with a British publishing house that produced educational books. As the months passed by, however, he became dissatisfied with his job and started looking for something new to do. In the meantime, he married Jane Elizabeth Oriel and started a family.

In 1952 Attenborough left his position with the publishing company in order to join the British Broadcasting Corporation (BBC), a public service organization that was England's primary provider of radio and television programming. Upon joining the BBC, Attenborough received training in producing television programs. He then spent the next few years helping to produce a number of weekly shows for the corporation's television station. "I produced political, quiz, and children's programs—shows of all types," he recalled.

Attenborough enjoyed working for the BBC, but he felt that much of the station's television programming was quite boring. With this in mind, he began thinking about new shows that might generate greater excitement from viewers. In 1954 Attenborough and Jack Lester, the London Zoo's curator of reptiles, came up with an idea for a new and innovative program designed to capitalize on the popularity of BBC shows about animals and nature.

Prior to the mid-1950s, the primary nature show on the BBC was a program called *Zootime*. "We used to get the curator of mammals from London Zoo to stuff some animals in a sack and bring them to the studio," recalled Attenborough. "People loved it because the animal would always

Attenborough shows a llama to a young visitor at the London Zoo, 1980.

bite the curator or pee on his trousers. Basically, that was the first natural history [program]."

Attenborough and Lester proposed a far more exciting and scientifically valuable version of *Zootime*. They wanted to launch a series of expeditions around the world to film exotic animals in their natural habitat and collect them for study. BBC administrators approved the idea for the series, which became known as *Zoo Quest*. In September 1954 Attenborough, Lester, and a film crew left for Africa to make the first episode of the series.

Beginning a Life of Adventure

The *Zoo Quest* crew's first adventure took place in Sierra Leone, a country in West Africa. Sierra Leone was home to a rare bird, Picarthartes gymnocephalus, that had never been shown in captivity or seen on its nest by any European. But Attenborough and the crew roamed deep into the wilderness in search of the elusive creature. As they pushed deeper into the jungle, Attenborough became overwhelmed by the natural beauty and variety of the region. The trip, he later said, "was a revelation of the splendor and fecundity of the natural world from which I have never recovered." It was also a tremendous success, for the group eventually found the bird and filmed it in its natural environment.

When *Zoo Quest* first began, Lester was chosen to serve as the narrator for the series. But illness soon prevented him from working on the program, and Attenborough took over the narration responsibilities. *Zoo Quest* marked the first time that he had ever appeared in front of the camera for the BBC, but he presented a friendly, enthusiastic, and bold image that proved very popular with English television viewers. As Timothy Green wrote in *Smithsonian*, Attenborough "appealed to armchair travelers who felt that here was a real explorer taking them along and sharing wildlife secrets, gamely brushing discomfort aside." Before long, both he and the *Zoo Quest* show were well-known throughout the country.

"[Animals are] easy things to make [television] programs about because they have everything going for them. They are amazingly beautiful; they are amazingly unpredictable—they're always doing things that you couldn't conceive that they would want to do, or be physically capable of doing—and there's always something new. . . . If you make the programs well, a child of five will watch them and a zoology professor of 80 will watch them; they are multilayered programs."

Attenborough worked on the *Zoo Quest* series as director, producer, writer, and narrator for the next ten years, from 1954 to 1964. During that time, he led expeditions deep into the most remote corners of the globe to capture footage of rare wildlife in its natural habitat. He made 48 documentary films from these trips. In addition, he wrote several books about his *Zoo Quest* adventures during this period, including *Zoo Quest for a Dragon* (1957), about the Komodo dragon lizards of Indonesia, and *Zoo Quest in Paraguay* (1959).

Years later, Attenborough remarked that the popularity of the *Zoo Quest* films and books did not surprise him. "[Animals are] easy things to make programs about because they have everything going for them," he said. "They are amazingly beautiful; they are amazingly unpredictable—they're always doing things that you couldn't conceive that they would want to do, or be physically capable of doing—and there's always something new.

They are not about economics, trade unionism, politics, or war, which seem to dominate the screen everywhere else. If you make the programs well, a child of five will watch them and a zoology professor of 80 will watch them; they are multilayered programs."

Becoming a Programming Executive at the BBC

In 1965 Attenborough accepted an offer to serve as head program director for BBC 2, a new, second television channel operated by the British Broadcasting Corporation. He spent the next four years at BBC 2, where he gained a reputation as an innovative and talented developer of television series and specials. Critically acclaimed shows that appeared on the station during this time ranged from history-oriented works like *Civilisation* and

The Ascent of Man to classical dramas such as *Henry the Eighth*. "I had total freedom [in that position]," recalled Attenborough. "It was terrific. The best job in television. It was entirely up to me to decide what we should do and what we shouldn't do."

"[Life on Earth] *achieves the emotional power of a cinematic poem," wrote reviewer Harry F. Waters in* Newsweek. "*[The program] is both a miraculous pageant and a major television epic.*"

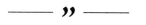

In 1969 Attenborough was named director of programming for both BBC channels. He excelled in his new duties, but his responsibilities made it impossible for him to pursue his interests in travel and natural history. This became a source of great unhappiness to him, and he finally resigned in 1972 so that he could return to documentary filmmaking and writing. "My moral fibre is not sufficiently strong enough to be able to go on doing things excellently I don't enjoy doing," he later explained. "The house was paid for, the piano bought, the children had left home. I'd done my bit as an administrator, but what I enjoy is making [documentary films]."

Achieving International Fame as a Filmmaker

After leaving the BBC, Attenborough began work on a major film project that examined art in primitive societies all around the world. He traveled over 25,000 miles during the next two years, exploring the artwork and history of cultures across the globe. "I was interested in the function of art in tribal societies," he explained. "Sculpture, painting, weaving, carving all have natural functions, but to understand their messages fully we have to know something about the artists who produced them, the society to which they belonged and the purposes for which they made them." In 1975 Attenborough's documentary, which he called *The Tribal Eye,* was shown on the BBC as a seven-part series. The film received warm praise from reviewers. It also was widely credited with boosting the popularity of an exhibition of primitive art that was being held at London's Museum of Mankind at the time of the broadcast.

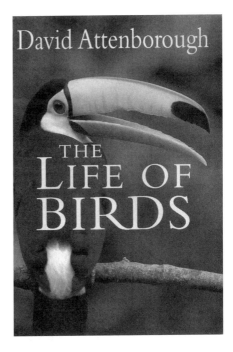

After completing *The Tribal Eye,* Attenborough turned his attention to an even more ambitious project. He decided that he wanted to make a documentary that would show the entire natural history of the Earth, including the evolution of all living creatures. In order to accomplish this, he assembled a talented filmmaking team and spent the next three years roaming across the planet. By the time filming on the project had been completed, Attenborough and his crew had traveled to more than 100 locations in 40 countries on every continent around the world. The filmmaker then spent the next several months editing the movie footage and writing the narration for the series, which was to be shown on BBC.

The documentary, called *Life on Earth,* was televised as a 13-part series in England in 1978. It was enormously popular, drawing an estimated 10 million viewers for each weekly episode. The film also received high praise from critics. They hailed Attenborough for the film's beautiful imagery and its engaging, easily understood language. Meanwhile, Attenborough published a book version of the documentary, also called *Life on Earth.* The book eventually sold over three million copies, and naturalist author Desmond Morris spoke for many reviewers when he called it "the best introduction to natural history ever written."

Attenborough was delighted with the public reaction to both the film and the book, which combined photographs with additional natural history information that was not featured in the documentary. "I couldn't just use my scripts to make a book," he later said. "The book has things in it that the film commentary just couldn't include. The material demanded another form, rethought and reshaped. I've always kept a daily journal in the field, and that was a great help in writing the book."

Life on Earth caused such a sensation in England that television stations in other European countries decided to broadcast the entire series. In 1982 the film was shown in the United States on the Public Broadcasting System (PBS), where it was both a popular and critical success. "[*Life on Earth*] achieves the emotional power of a cinematic poem," wrote reviewer Harry F. Waters in *Newsweek*. "[The program] is both a miraculous pageant and a major television epic." Together, the *Life on Earth* film and book made Attenborough famous around the world. But he remained modest about his accomplishments and thankful for his good fortune. "I'm the luckiest man," he stated. "I go to the most marvelous places in the world and I'm paid for it."

Studying Ecosystems around the World

In 1983 Attenborough released *Spirit of Asia,* a documentary film series on Asian culture, art, and religion. As with many of his other film projects, he released a book version on the same subject at the same time. Two years later, he completed another documentary project, called *The Living Planet: A Portrait of the Earth.* In this series, which Attenborough viewed as a sequel to *Life on Earth,* the filmmaker set out to examine all the various ecosystems—unique environmental regions—that exist around the world. In addition, he explored the ways in which various creatures have adapted to those environments in order to survive. "What we couldn't do in the other series [*Life on Earth*] is show the way in which birds and reptiles interrelate, communities characteristic of a particular environment," Attenborough explained. "This new program looks at one group of environments worldwide [in each episode]—one [show] about deserts, another about grasslands, and individual shows about jungles and coastlines and mountains."

Attenborough developed the series as a tool to help people of all ages learn about the wonderful and complex ecosystems that cover the world. But he also expressed a hope that *The Living Planet* would teach people to "recognize first of all that the natural world is the source of our riches, our food, our spiritual delight. That it is immensely complicated and that it is very vulnerable. And that if we recognize that everything worthwhile comes from the natural world to us, that we have the power over it, then maybe we'll come to our senses and handle it properly."

In 1987 Attenborough completed yet another massive film project. Like his earlier works, *The First Eden* was shown first on the BBC, then broadcast in countries all around the world, including the United States. This documentary series examined the history of the Mediterranean Sea and its earliest human inhabitants. The Mediterranean is an inland sea that is bordered by southern Europe, western Asia, and northern Africa, and linked to the Atlantic Ocean at its western end by the Strait of Gibraltar. Many of mankind's earliest civilizations first developed along its shores. "This area has been continually inhabited by humans for the longest time," stated Attenborough. "It's where humans domesticated animals and created great civilizations. In the Mediterranean, an entire cycle has been completed of humans moving into an area, exploiting and exhausting the natural resources, destroying the area, and moving on. This area has blatant examples of erosion, pollution, and extinction. Much of what happened here foreshadows the ecological dilemmas of the modern world."

"I hope my work has helped people become more aware of nature and the Earth. I have always thought an education in the natural sciences illuminates your life forever. You can't be a natural scientist without acquiring a profound reverence for nature. Everyone has that reverence; it's just that some of us lose sight of it. We can't let that happen. We would be deprived of so much."

The First Eden was hailed by critics and television audiences alike for its informative blend of natural history and environmental study. "A major theme of *The First Eden*," wrote *Earth Science* contributor Louise J. Fisher, "is that nature has never failed to support people, but people have failed to support nature." Attenborough, meanwhile, argued that natural history and the environment are closely linked. "I hope my work has helped people become more aware of nature and the Earth," he said. "I have always thought an education in the natural sciences illuminates your life forever. You can't be a natural scientist without acquiring a profound reverence for nature. Everyone has that reverence; it's just that some of us lose sight of it. We can't let that happen. We would be deprived of so much."

In 1990 Attenborough added to his worldwide reputation with *The Trials of Life*. The filmmaker described this documentary as the third and final film in a trilogy that included his classics *Life on Earth* and *The Living Planet*. It concentrated on animal behavior and on the aspects of life that confront animals as they progress from birth to death, including propagating, caring

Attenborough with a golden eagle from The Life of Birds, *1999.*

for the young, finding food, making a home, socializing, fighting, migrating, communicating, and courting and mating. This 12-hours series was praised for its visually stunning camera work and for its informative and fascinating subject matter. Three years later, he released *Life in the Freezer,* a documentary that studied the many creatures who make their homes in the harsh world of Antarctica.

Attenborough continued to serve as director and producer of these film projects. But he remained best known for his on-screen role as the friendly and knowledgeable narrator who guides audiences through each film. In fact, his enthusiastic style, honed over three decades of documentary film work, has made him one of England's most recognized television personalities. "[Attenborough] has the ability of the very best TV presenters to infect you with his own love of his subject or, more correctly, with his own astonishment," explained Mark Edwards in *The Sunday Times.* "Part of Attenborough is still the schoolboy collecting fossils. We watch to connect with and perhaps to envy a man with such a passion for his work."

Producing Documentaries on Plants and Birds

During the mid-1990s Attenborough began work on a new documentary project on the subject of plants. When he first announced the project, many people wondered how even a man of Attenborough's talents could make an interesting film on a subject that seemed so unsuited for television. But the filmmaker used time-lapse photography and other innovations to create the fascinating 1995 documentary called *The Private Life of Plants*. In some cases, Attenborough compressed a week of a plant's life into 20 seconds of footage. As a result, noted Jim Bawden in the *Toronto Star*, "You see Arctic poppies tracking the sun, carnivorous plants contorting into traps for unwary prey, parasitic vines stalking an enemy. Squirting cucumbers fire off their seeds like rockets."

In 1998, Attenborough released a documentary on the history and development of birds around the world. *The Life of Birds,* which took the naturalist three years to make and for which he traveled to 42 different countries, was praised by critics for both its educational and entertainment value. *Chicago Tribune* contributor Stevenson Swanson commented that "with characteristic thoroughness, the series presents the wide variety of ways in which birds deal with the challenges they face: why most birds fly and some don't, how they find food, how they find a mate, . . . [and] how they raise their young." *Newsday*, meanwhile, called the film "a near- hypnotic viewing experience that is filled with some of the most spectacular nature photography many viewers will have ever seen."

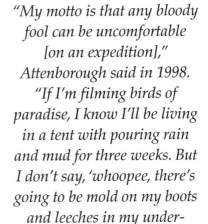

——— " ———

"My motto is that any bloody fool can be uncomfortable [on an expedition]," Attenborough said in 1998. *"If I'm filming birds of paradise, I know I'll be living in a tent with pouring rain and mud for three weeks. But I don't say, 'whoopee, there's going to be mold on my boots and leeches in my underpants.' I'm never lonely. I love the people I work with."*

——— " ———

Attenborough released *The Life of Birds* at the age of 72, when few naturalists of his generation still venture out into the wild. But the veteran filmmaker refuses to consider retirement. He admits that he can no longer do some of the things he did as a young man, but he still enjoys being out in the wilderness doing what he loves. "My motto is that any bloody fool can be uncomfortable [on an expedition]," he said in 1998. "If I'm filming birds of paradise, I know I'll be living in a tent with pouring rain and mud for three weeks. But I don't say, 'whoopee, there's going to be mold on my boots and leeches in my underpants.' I'm never lonely. I love the people I work with."

Attenborough on Easter Island.

Recent Work

Attenborough recently completed *The Lost Gods of Easter Island* (2000). In this one-hour documentary, he changed his usual role from that of explorer to historical detective—all because of an interesting artifact. Some 15 years ago, he had attended an auction where he saw a wood carving of a person with "a grotesque head, attached to a body grossly elongated and as thin as a stick." The auction catalogue indicated that the figure was originally from Easter Island, an island in the South Pacific about 2,200 miles off the coast of Chile. Easter Island is famous for its hieroglyphs and its monolithic statues of people, carved from volcanic rock. There are about 600 statues, called *moai* (pronounced MO-eye), scattered around the island. They range in height from 10 to 40 feet, and some weigh more than 50 tons. There have been many different theories in recent years about who carved these huge statues and when and how they were carved—by island natives, by Incans from Peru, by giants, by visitors from outer space—but no one knows for sure.

At the auction, Attenborough was intrigued by this wood carving that resembled the *moai* of Easter Island. "The auctioneers clearly thought it was of no consequence," he recalls, "carved perhaps in recent times, made maybe to sell to visitors—a kind of early tourist piece—for they estimated its value as tiny compared with what a genuine early piece would be worth." The auction house knew only that the sculpture had come from a junk shop in Pennsylvania. So Attenborough purchased the carving and began to investigate it, trying to determine what it represented, who had carved it, and where and when it was done. His investigation ended up circling the globe, from Russia to Australia to England and back to Easter Island. That investigation forms the starting point for *The Lost Gods of Easter Island*, which uses art, myth, anthropology, history, religion, and natural history to trace the origin of the carving and tell the story of a people and their culture.

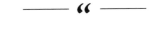

"[Attenborough] has the ability of the very best TV presenters to infect you with his own love of his subject or, more correctly, with his own astonishment. Part of Attenborough is still the schoolboy collecting fossils. We watch to connect with and perhaps to envy a man with such a passion for his work."– Mark Edwards, The Sunday Times

MARRIAGE AND FAMILY

In 1950 Attenborough married Jane Elizabeth Ebsworth Oriel, whom he met in Leicester as a teenager. They had two children, Susan and Robert. Their marriage lasted for 47 years, until she died of a sudden brain hemorrhage in 1997. Attenborough continues to live in Richmond, Surrey, England, where he and his wife raised their family.

HOBBIES AND OTHER INTERESTS

Attenborough enjoys listening to classical music and is an accomplished classical piano player. He also collects ethnic and tribal art and curiosities from all over the world. In addition, he is a longtime member of numerous environmental and scientific organizations. For example, he has been a member of the Nature Conservancy Council since 1973, and a trustee of the British Museum since 1980.

DOCUMENTARIES

Life on Earth, 1979
Spirit of Asia, 1983
The Living Planet, 1984
The First Eden: The Mediterranean World and Man, 1987
The Trials of Life, 1990
Life in the Freezer, 1993
The Private Life of Plants, 1995
Attenborough in Paradise, 1996
The Life of Birds, 1998
The Lost Gods of Easter Island, 2000

WRITINGS

Zoo Quest to Guiana, 1956
Zoo Quest for a Dragon, 1957
Zoo Quest in Paraguay, 1959
Quest in Paradise, 1960
People of Paradise, 1961
Zoo Quest to Madagascar, 1961 (also published as *Bridge to the Past: Animals and People of Madagascar,* 1962)
Quest under Capricorn, 1963
My Favorite Stories of Exploration, 1964 (editor)
David Attenborough's Fabulous Animals, 1975 (with Molly Cox)
The Tribal Eye, 1976
Life on Earth: A Natural History, 1979
Journeys to the Past: Travels in New Guinea, Madagascar, and the Northern Territory of Australia, 1981
Discovering Life on Earth: A Natural History, 1981
The Zoo Quest Expeditions (contains *Zoo Quest to Guiana, Zoo Quest for a Dragon,* and *Zoo Quest in Paraguay*), 1982
The Spirit of Asia, 1983 (with Michael MacIntyre)
The Living Planet: A Portrait of the Earth, 1984
The First Eden: The Mediterranean World and Man, 1987
The Atlas of the Living World, 1989

The Trials of Life: A Natural History of Animal Behavior, 1990
The Private Life of Plants, 1995
The Life of Birds, 1998

HONORS AND AWARDS

Silver Medal (Zoological Society of London): 1966
Silver Medal (Royal Television Society): 1966
Desmond Davis Award (Society of Film and Television Arts): 1970
Cherry Kearton Medal (Royal Geographical Society): 1972
Commander of the British Empire: 1974
Fellowship Award (British Academy of Film and Television Arts): 1980
Kalinga Prize (UNESCO): 1982
Companion of Honour for Distinguished Service: 1995
Natural History Book Award: 1998, for *The Life of Birds* (book)
Peabody Award: 1999, for *The Life of Birds* (film)

FURTHER READING

Books

Contemporary Authors, New Revision Series, Vol. 6, 1982; Vol. 30, 1990
Environment Encyclopedia and Directory, 1994
Langley, Andrew. *The Making of "The Living Planet,"* 1985
Who's Who, 1999
Writer's Directory, 1996

Periodicals

Chicago Tribune, Aug. 25, 1999, Tempo section, p.1
Christian Science Monitor, Dec. 7, 1984, p.39; Aug. 22, 1985, p.23
Current Biography 1983
Earth Science, Fall 1987, p.11
Life, Feb. 1982, p.23
Los Angeles Times, Oct. 30, 1987, Calendar section, p.29; June 27, 1999,
   Calendar section, p.3
New Statesman, Dec. 18, 1998, p.28
New York Times, Jan. 27, 1985, Section 2, p.25
Newsday, July 18, 1999, p.D15
Newsweek, Feb. 1, 1982
People, Feb. 8, 1982, p.105
Smithsonian, Nov. 1981, p.134

Sunday Times (London), Feb. 20, 1994
Toronto Star, Nov. 15, 1987, p.D5; Oct. 7, 1995, p.SW3

ADDRESS

BBC
Wood Lane
London, England W12 0TT

WORLD WIDE WEB SITES

http://www.pbs.org/lifeofbirds
http://www.wwf-uk.org/news/attenbor.htm

Robert Ballard 1942-
American Oceanographer and Explorer
Discovered the *Titanic* Shipwreck
Founded the JASON Project

BIRTH

Robert Duane Ballard was born on June 30, 1942, in Wichita, Kansas, but he grew up in California. His parents were Chester Patrick Ballard, an aerospace executive who helped build the first supersonic jets, and Harriett Nell (May) Ballard. Ballard has one brother, Richard, who was born two years before him. He also has a younger sister, Nancy.

YOUTH

Robert Ballard's lifelong interest in ocean exploration can be traced back to his early childhood, when he spent endless hours exploring the beaches and harbors near his southern California home. "As long as I can remember, I've been fascinated by the sea," remembers Ballard. "As a boy . . . I was always collecting shells and driftwood that the ocean washed up on the beaches. I also loved to watch the creatures that lived underwater in tidal pools. As a teenager, instead of becoming a surfer like most of my friends, I took up scuba diving and began to explore the world just beneath the ocean surface."

> "As long as I can remember, I've been fascinated by the sea. As a boy . . . I was always collecting shells and driftwood that the ocean washed up on the beaches. I also loved to watch the creatures that lived underwater in tidal pools. As a teenager, instead of becoming a surfer like most of my friends, I took up scuba diving and began to explore the world just beneath the ocean surface."

As Ballard grew older, his parents also regularly took their children to the Scripps Institution of Oceanography, a facility just north of their home in San Diego that featured a public aquarium and educational exhibits. Young Robert loved the Scripps aquarium, and he passed many afternoons watching sharks, octopi, tropical fish, manta rays, and other exotic sea creatures as they swam in their watery tanks.

When Ballard was not roaming the beach or the grounds of the Scripps Institution, he could often be found reading in his room or some other quiet corner of the house. He was particularly fond of reading about the lives of real-life explorers like Osa and Martin Johnson, whose expeditions to the South Pacific and Africa in the 1930s and 1940s were recounted in a series of popular books. "When I was a kid, Osa and Martin Johnson were my idols," Ballard later said. But his favorite book was Jules Verne's classic fantasy *20,000 Leagues Under the Sea.* This story, about a mysterious scientist named Captain Nemo who roams the world in a spectacular submarine of his own invention, was one that Ballard read over and over again.

In 1953 the Ballard family moved from San Diego to Downey, California, part of the Los Angeles metropolitan area. By this time, Robert's sister

Nancy had been diagnosed with a birth defect that prevented her from developing the ability to speak. News of this birth defect saddened the Ballards, but Robert's parents rallied the family together and arranged activities in which all their children could participate. They organized family camping trips deep into the mountains and sailing and snorkeling trips around islands along the California coastline. The family even named their cruising boat the *Nancy Ann* in honor of its youngest member.

Years later, Ballard said that his sister's handicap profoundly influenced his own attitude toward life when he was growing up. "Knowing Nancy would never be able to go out in the world and lead a 'normal' life made me twice as determined to make the most of my opportunities," he recalled. "I had this strong sense, even as a fairly young kid, that because I had been blessed with health and intelligence, it would have been sinful to squander these gifts. Nancy's handicap gave me a sense of urgency."

EDUCATION AND MILITARY SERVICE

Ballard was a good student who was popular with his classmates. He also emerged as a terrific athlete at Downey High School, where he starred in football, basketball, and tennis. But despite the demands of practice and homework and his busy social life, he still found time to slip into the Pacific Ocean in his scuba diving gear on a regular basis. "To me, going to sea was the most natural thing in the world," he remarked. "When I opened my eyes, I didn't see amber waves of grain, I saw the sea."

After completing his junior year in high school, Ballard gained admittance into a summer internship program at the Scripps Institution of Oceanography, where he had spent many happy afternoons as a youngster. Ballard spent the next three months helping out on a wide range of research activities at Scripps. He even spent several weeks out at sea on research boats, assisting in water sample collection and other experiments. On one of those voyages, his ship was caught in a wicked storm that tossed the vessel about for three straight days, nearly sinking it at one point. The storm shattered many of the boat's windows, injured a couple of crewmen, and caused widespread seasickness. But despite this frightening display of the ocean's power, Ballard returned home determined to pursue a career at sea.

Ballard graduated from Downey High School in 1960 and enrolled at the University of California at Santa Barbara. During his time on the Santa Barbara campus, he seemed to participate in every possible extracurricular activity, from intramural sports to student politics (he served as president of his class during his junior year).

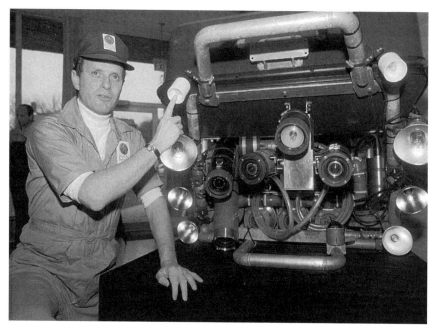

Ballard points out features of Jason, *a new underwater robot, at Woods Hole, Massachusetts, 1988.*

Ballard also went through the U.S. Army's Reserve Officers Training Corps (ROTC) program during this time. The ROTC program prepares young people to serve as officers in the U.S. military. Ballard excelled in ROTC, rising to the rank of deputy brigade commander of his unit during his senior year. After completing his ROTC work, he became a member of the Army Reserve. The reserves are people with military training who can be called to active duty in case of war or other national emergencies.

In 1965, Ballard graduated from the University of California, Santa Barbara, with a bachelor's degree in science. He then began working toward a graduate degree in marine geology at the University of Hawaii. Ballard spent 1965 and 1966 at Hawaii, where he earned extra money as a part-time dolphin trainer at Sea Life Park. "I spent hours teaching dolphins to dive through hoops and perform other tricks," he remembered. During this time, he also transferred from the Army Reserve to the Navy Reserve.

In 1966 Ballard married Marjorie Hargas and transferred to the University of Southern California to continue his studies. But a year later, the Navy ordered him to appear for active military duty. This order had been given erroneously, because men in the reserves were allowed to avoid active duty as long as they pursued their college education. But Ballard did not fight the order. Instead, he reported to the Office of Naval Research (ONR) in Boston, Massachusetts. His primary responsibility when he arrived at the ONR was to monitor organizations that were undertaking scientific research programs funded by the Navy.

Ballard and his wife arrived in Boston in March 1967. He served the ONR as an oceanographic liaison officer for the next two and a half years, eventually rising to the rank of lieutenant. But he actually spent most of this time as part of a submarine research group at Woods Hole Oceanographic Institution in nearby Woods Hole, Massachusetts. His inclusion in this submarine research effort gave Ballard an opportunity to work at an institute that was known worldwide for its studies on oceans and marine life. This assignment was a lucky break, and he was determined to make the most of it. He devoted himself to learning all that he could about submarine technology and the ocean from the brilliant scientific staff at Woods Hole.

In September 1969 the Navy released Ballard from active duty. The Woods Hole Oceanographic Institution quickly hired him as a research associate in ocean engineering. The institute also offered to pay for him to return to school and earn his Ph.D. Ballard happily accepted the generous offer. He spent the next four years dividing his time between raising a family, working for Woods Hole, and attending graduate courses in oceanography at the nearby University of Rhode Island. In 1974 he earned his Ph.D. in oceanography from Rhode Island after completing a dissertation, a lengthy research paper required for graduation. He wrote his dissertation on the theory of plate tectonics, a scientific theory that the earth's crust consists of several major plates that move slowly over time.

CAREER HIGHLIGHTS

Using Submarines as Scientific Tools

After leaving the Navy, Ballard remained with the Woods Hole Oceanographic Institution because it was engaged in so many exciting ocean research projects. In fact, he remained affiliated with Woods Hole for the next 27 years, from 1970 to 1997. During that time, he emerged as the world's most famous deep-ocean explorer.

Ballard's first taste of glory came in the early 1970s, when he worked as a member of Woods Hole's *Alvin* team. *Alvin* was a small three-man submarine used for underwater exploration, and Ballard believed that this vehicle and others like it could be valuable scientific tools. In the early 1970s, though, many members of the scientific community did not agree. "There were quite a few people . . . who felt that submarines were expensive toys that geologists played with, and that no real good science would come out of them," he said.

Ballard became fascinated by the **Titanic** *after he became friends with Bill Tantum, the head of the* **Titanic** *Historical Society. "I would sit and listen for hours as he told me the spellbinding story of what had happened the night she sank," Ballard said. "Together we would talk about my dream of finding her. The* **Titanic** *began to mean more to me than simply a challenging target to find in the deep ocean. This greatest of all sea disasters soon gripped me as a fascinating and moving human drama. Now the* **Titanic** *had me completely under her spell."*

In 1973 Ballard was given his first opportunity to prove the doubters wrong. Based on his extensive diving experience with the *Alvin*, he received a spot on Project FAMOUS (French-American Mid-Ocean Underseas Study). The mission of this two-year project was to study a 60-square-mile section of the Atlantic Ocean floor using the most advanced scientific technology. As it turned out, Ballard proved to be one of the most valuable members of the entire project. He designed a deep sea remote-control survey vessel called *Angus* that could take pictures at tremendous depths. This submarine became a vital tool in the project's overall success. In fact, the performance of the *Angus* greatly heightened his credentials as a bright young scientist and a skilled submarine operator.

In 1976 Ballard was named chief scientist for another major French-American ocean research expedition. This mission targeted the Cayman Trough, a canyon located at the bottom of the Atlantic Ocean just south of Cuba that is 24,000 feet deep. As a point of comparison, Mount Everest, the highest mountain in the world, is 29,000 feet high. During this expedition to the Cayman Trough, Ballard and his fellow scientists used the *Alvin* and other submarines to make the first accurate map of the region. They also found evidence of recent volcanic activity on the bottom and collected the deepest rock samples ever taken from the sea floor.

One year later, Ballard joined the Galapagos Hydrothermal Expedition, a scientific mission to investigate unusual water temperature variations off the Galapagos Islands near the coast of Ecuador. A short time after arriving in the region, the group learned that hydrothermal vents (spouts of mineral-rich water) dotted the sea floor, accounting for the changes in water temperature. But as they looked at pictures taken by Ballard's *Angus* submarine, they were amazed to learn that the minerals from these hydrothermal vents apparently supported an array of marine life, including large communities of crabs, giant clams, and eight-foot long tube worms.

This discovery excited the members of the expedition, and in 1979 Ballard led a return trip to the Galapagos area to undertake a more detailed study. During this visit, the scientific team discovered a series of underwater vents called "black smokers," a type of underwater volcano that belched extremely hot fluids up from chimneys of lava located on the ocean floor. All around these vents were large colonies of strange, previously unknown sea creatures that fed on the rich minerals found in these waters. Ballard's findings stunned marine biologists, who had not believed that any creatures could survive at such depths. "[The Galapagos trip] was an incredible emotional roller-coaster ride," Ballard recalled. "And it made me realize that my honest motivation is as much the excitement of exploration as the science of it."

Developing the *Argo-Jason* Submarines

By 1980, Ballard noted that "I had spent more hours in the deep ocean than any other scientist." In addition, he had became a valuable contributor to the National Geographic Society and its documentary specials and magazine. All of these factors combined to make him one of the best known oceanographers in the world.

Ballard's international reputation enabled him to pursue exciting new ideas in undersea exploration. In 1981 he established the Deep Submergence Laboratory at Woods Hole with assistance from the U.S. Navy and the National Science Foundation. This facility gave him the tools he needed to develop a new generation of unmanned, remotely operated submarine vehicles that would allow researchers to maneuver from the safety of surface ships or land. Ballard believed that the development of these unmanned robot vehicles would have great scientific value, because they would allow humankind to explore the most remote depths of the oceans without risking human lives.

The final result of Ballard's efforts was the *Argo-Jason* system. The *Argo* was a deep-sea automated submarine with three video cameras that could see

Ballard and a student Argonaut from the JASON Project broadcast live to share their experiences in Peru with students around the world.

in almost total darkness. *Jason* was a smaller, self-propelled robot that could detach from the Argo and investigate objects by using special mechanical arms. Once he completed work on the *Argo* and the *Jason,* Ballard began to ponder various projects that would allow him to put them to good use. Before long, he decided that he would use his new submarines to look for the *Titanic,* the most famous shipwreck in history.

Searching for the *Titanic*

The *Titanic* was a British steamship that sank in the North Atlantic on April 15, 1912, on its maiden voyage to America. The luxury liner had been described by its makers and owners as "unsinkable," but a collision with an iceberg opened a huge gash along its side. Some passengers managed to escape the sinking vessel on lifeboats, but more than 1,500 people died in the disaster. The tragedy stunned the world and became the most famous maritime disaster in history. Several expeditions to find the sunken vessel were eventually launched, but none succeeded.

Ballard had always been fascinated by the *Titanic* tragedy, and he began to think about launching an expedition to find the ship. His interest in the ship became even more intense after he became friends with Bill Tantum, the head of the *Titanic* Historical Society. "I would sit and listen for hours as he told me the spellbinding story of what had happened the night she sank," Ballard said. "Together we would talk about my dream of finding her. The *Titanic* began to mean more to me than simply a challenging target to find in the deep ocean. This greatest of all sea disasters soon gripped me as a fascinating and moving human drama. Now the *Titanic* had me completely under her spell."

In 1984 Ballard decided to use his new *Argo-Jason* system to undertake a search for the doomed luxury liner. "My idea was to pursue her remains in the spirit of exploration," he stated. "A kind of coming together of science and history." He joined forces with a team of French scientists and secured funding and assistance for the expedition from the U.S. Navy. One year later, in July 1985, Ballard's French colleagues arrived at the last-known location of the Titanic and initiated a sonar sweep of the area. Ballard arrived a few weeks later on the *Knorr,* a U.S. Navy research vessel, with both the *Argo* and *Angus* submarines on board.

"I knew it wasn't going to be easy [to find the *Titanic*]," recalled Ballard. "The terrain in that area is very complex. In 1929, some 17 years after the *Titanic* sank, the area had the biggest earthquake ever recorded underwater. It triggered an avalanche of moving mud about the size of all of New England. We worried that perhaps *Titanic* was buried beneath this great landslide. We had all sorts of worries." In addition, the expedition's boats were rocked by strong currents and fierce storms as they bobbed in the middle of the North Atlantic. As the days ticked by with no sign of the *Titanic,* Ballard secretly began to wonder if their mission would end in failure.

In late August, the French ship left the area and returned home. Ballard stayed, however, and continued the search using his *Argo-Jason* and *Angus* submarines. Early in the morning of September 1, 1985, Ballard's perseverance paid off. He was awakened from a restless sleep by a crew member who told him that his crew had spotted something interesting down on the ocean floor. Ballard rushed to the *Knorr's* command center. He found his team gathered around a video screen that transmitted images from the *Argo,* which was prowling the ocean bottom thousands of feet below them. At first the screen showed only sand and rock, but then a boiler from the *Titanic* suddenly came into view. The scientists and crew on the *Knorr* exploded in celebration. After all, they had just found the most famous shipwreck in history. But after several moments of wild celebration, they all realized that it was almost 2:00 a.m., the hour when the *Titanic* had sank 73 years before. Ballard subsequently led everyone out onto the deck of the

Knorr, where they held a moment of silence in memory of those who had perished on the ship.

Ballard and his team spent the next eight days exploring the *Titanic*. During this time, the video cameras of the *Argo* and the *Angus* captured valuable footage of the ship's exterior. They also filmed images of hundreds of artifacts that sank with the ship, including bottles of wine, china plates, and personal effects. During this period, Ballard was particularly affected by underwater footage of the ship's empty lifeboat cranes. "To me that was the symbolism of the *Titanic*," he later said. "They were what all the people who died saw as they were looking for a lifeboat. . . . And there it was in the picture. We came up over the top of that with *Argo*, saw the picture, and—Bang!— it was like a sock to my stomach."

> **"**
>
> *When Ballard saw the* **Titanic** *in underwater video images sent from the submarine* **Argo**, *he was particularly affected by footage of the ship's empty lifeboat cranes. "To me that was the symbolism of the* **Titanic**. *They were what all the people who died saw as they were looking for a lifeboat. . . . And there it was in the picture. We came up over the top of that with* **Argo**, *saw the picture, and—Bang!— it was like a sock to my stomach."*
>
> **"**

Returning as an International Celebrity

Ballard's discovery instantly transformed him into a worldwide celebrity. When he returned to the United States in September 1985, he was greeted with celebrations and a blizzard of requests for interviews. People all around the world wanted to hear the story of his quest and learn about the condition of the famous ship. "The *Titanic* lies now in 13,000 feet of water on a gently sloping Alpine-looking countryside overlooking a small canyon below," he reported. "Its bow faces north. The ship sits upright on its bottom with its mighty stacks pointed upward. There is no light at this great depth and little life can be found. It is a quiet and peaceful place—and a fitting place for the remains of this greatest of sea tragedies to rest. Forever may it remain that way. And may God bless these now-found souls."

In 1986 Ballard made a follow-up visit to the *Titanic* wreck site to conduct further research on the state of the ship. He refused to take any of the

Ballard joins two student Argonauts as they prepare for a live JASON Project broadcast from NASA's Johnson Space Center in Houston, Texas.

ship's artifacts, saying that the boat should be left undisturbed out of respect for those who perished on the ship. But he left two memorials on the *Titanic,* one from the Explorers Club and another from the *Titanic* Historical Society. One year later, he published *Discovery of the Titanic,* a bestseller about his achievement.

Some scientists griped about Ballard's new high profile. They charged that his book and his willingness to give television interviews and lectures showed that he was a publicity hound. But Ballard defended his decision to write books and articles for the general public. "Since all my writings deal with expeditions I am conducting in the deep sea, the writing process has become a part of an epic journey which now seems incomplete unless I return from an important expedition to report its findings."

Ballard also pointed out that famous scientists like Carl Sagan and Jacques Cousteau often used lectures and television appearances to generate excitement about their areas of scientific research. "[Sagan and Cousteau] have probably lost some of the regard of their fellow scientists," Ballard admitted. "But look at the good they've done by making science exciting and making people aware of it! And don't forget that my science is paid for by some poor coal miner whose taxes go to support me while I'm having fun, so I feel it's responsible to go to him and [other members of] the public and tell them what I'm doing." Finally, Ballard observed that funding for future scientific research depended on the continued support of the general public. "If we want more money, we're going to have to fight for it and convince the populace that science is important. We can't just sit in our ivory tower and say they don't appreciate us."

Looking for New Challenges in Exploration

Ballard's discovery of the *Titanic* had been a great triumph. But he viewed it as only the beginning of an exciting new era in ocean research. "To me, the finding of the *Titanic* has two meanings," he said. "It is epilogue: an ending to the unfinished maiden voyage [of the *Titanic*]. But it is also prologue: the beginning of a new era in exploration. The *Titanic* is the first pyramid to be found in the deep sea. There are thousands of others, waiting to tell their tales."

Ballard also announced that he intended to seek out new challenges on the high seas. "I am an explorer who's a geologist," he said. "I'm an explorer who loves the ocean. And I'm an explorer who loves technology. To be an explorer I had to be a scientist. I love science. I love the pursuit of anything, and the pursuit of truth is very noble."

In 1988 Ballard launched a mission to find the *Bismarck,* a famous World War II German warship that had sunk in the Atlantic Ocean in May 1941 after a clash with British battleships. When he first set out for the general site where the *Bismarck* had been vanquished, the expedition failed. But he returned the following summer, and in June 1989 Ballard located the ship using the *Argo* and other sophisticated scientific tools. He found the warship at a depth of 15,000 feet, about 600 miles off the coast of France. Ballard reported that the ship was "in an excellent state of preservation," but he told the world that he had no plans to "salvage" the vessel by taking cargo or other materials from the wreck.

Creating the JASON Project

Ballard's successful quest for the *Bismarck* marked the explorer's first effort to involve students directly in his research missions. After that, he went on to create a program called the JASON Project. This program was designed to increase young people's interest in science by providing them with the opportunity to work directly with scientists on projects at sites around the world. Student participants in the JASON Project can watch special live broadcasts of scientific expeditions. They can also ask scientists questions via satellite and operate remote-control underwater probes.

"The JASON Project is really a voyage of discovery for educational motivation," said Ballard, who complains that most television shows portray scientists as geeks and wimps. "How can you possibly attract kids into science and engineering if their role model is a wimp? . . . We wanted, in our way, to begin to reshape that image by showing kids the excitement of exploration. That it is, in some sense, an athletic contest—that it has all the excitement and more than most of the professions."

The Project's ultimate purpose, Ballard added, is "to involve kids in an epic journey . . . in memory of Jason and the Argonauts who were the first Western explorers. The kids will actually be on the journey; some at sea with us, but most at replicas of our control center. They will see what we see when we see it. And we'll react when we discover things, which will show the kids that we (scientists) are just as human as they are. . . . Exploration and science in the sea are still in the Lewis and Clark phase. We now stand at the threshold of entering the deep sea; we have seen less than one-tenth of one percent of the planet beneath the ocean. We know more about the mountain ranges on Mars than we do about the mountain ranges beneath our own oceans. [But] technology has opened the door."

Ballard complains that most television shows portray scientists as geeks and wimps, and he started the JASON Project to counteract that image. "How can you possibly attract kids into science and engineering if their role model is a wimp? . . . We wanted, in our way, to begin to reshape that image by showing kids the excitement of exploration. That it is, in some sense, an athletic contest—that it has all the excitement and more than most of the professions."

Since 1989, Ballard has organized a JASON Project every year. These programs have enabled students to learn about science and history all around the world—underwater, on land, and in space. In 1989, for example, the JASON I Project discovered the first hydrothermal vents in the Mediterranean Sea, examined an ancient Roman shipwreck, and retrieved artifacts from under 2,100 feet of water. In 1990, JASON II explored the wrecks of two naval warships from the War of 1812, the *Hamilton* and the

Ballard next to the Amazon River in Peru for the JASON Project, 1999.

Scourge, at the bottom of Lake Ontario. The JASON IV Project of 1993, meanwhile, studied tropical ecosystems and coral reefs of the Caribbean around the Sea of Cortez. And the JASON VII Project of 1996 studied dolphins, manatees, sharks, coral reefs, and other creatures that make their home in Florida's waters. Other JASON Projects have gone to Belize, Hawaii, Florida, Iceland, and Wyoming's Yellowstone National Park over the years.

The current project, JASON XII, is called "Hawaii: A Living Laboratory." For this project, Ballard and a team of JASON researchers will explore these isolated islands, shaped by 30 million years of volcanic activity. The project will look at the islands' geological phenomena, as well as their diverse peoples and cultures. From there, the project will go on to examine the role that volcanoes play on land, in the sea, and throughout the solar system.

Ballard loves the JASON Project, which now broadcasts live over the Internet every year. He estimates that more than five million children from the United States, the United Kingdom, and Mexico participated in the program in its first decade, and he expects to reach millions more in the coming years. Certainly, the project has proven very popular with students. "Being down there is great," said one student who participated in JASON research work in Belize. "You're actually part of science. It was the greatest experience of my life. The JASON program has definitely made me want to have a career in science, and help humanity the way Bob has done."

Searching for Other Famous Shipwrecks

In addition to the JASON Project, Ballard has continued other work as well. In 1990 he agreed to serve as host of *National Geographic Explorer,* a weekly program produced by the National Geographic Society. But these new duties did not prevent him from continuing his life of exploration.

In 1992 Ballard went to the South Pacific island of Guadalcanal, where some of the fiercest battles of World War II were waged. During his expedition, he located a whole fleet of Japanese, American, and Australian warships that had been sunk in the area during the war. He located and identified 13 warships, including many of the most famous warships that were lost during that conflict. "There's more history preserved in the deep sea than in all the museums of the world combined," Ballard declared.

In 1993 Ballard led an expedition to explore the wreck of the *Lusitania.* This unarmed passenger liner had been sunk by a German submarine off the coast of Ireland on May 7, 1915, during World War I. The attack, which came without warning and claimed nearly 1,200 lives, triggered shock and outrage around the world when it occurred.

Unlike other ships that Ballard had targeted, the *Lusitania*'s final resting place was known. But Ballard used advanced robots and photographic equipment to provide the most detailed documentation yet of the ship's condition. He also wrote a book about the experience called *Exploring the Lusitania* (1995). As with his other books, it was popular with general readers and critics alike. The *London Daily Mail,* for example, said that it "reads like a fast-moving adventure story" with "pictures [that] are eerily moving, poignantly beautiful evocations of one of the wonders of the deep that would clearly take your breath away if you were to see it."

Founding the Institute for Exploration

In 1997 Ballard retired from his position as senior scientist at the Woods Hole Oceanographic Institution. But his retirement did not mean that he was done roaming the world's seas. In fact, the day after his retirement from Woods Hole he announced his decision to build his own Institute for Exploration in Mystic, Connecticut (it opened one year later). In late 1997, meanwhile, the blockbuster film *Titanic* was released. Ballard said he loved the movie, which triggered a renewal of interest in his discovery of the doomed ship.

> "The interesting thing about exploration of the sea is that it follows the classic pattern of the epic journey. You leave, go out and meet the elements — the dragon — and fight some sort of adversary. Then you attain truth, the pot of gold, and bring that back, pull up the drawbridge and lick your wounds. It's a quest."

Since launching the Institute for Exploration, Ballard has continued to display his talent for finding noteworthy shipwrecks. In 1997 he announced that he had discovered eight ancient sailing ships from the Roman and Phoenician empires deep in the Mediterranean Sea. Some of the vessels were more than 2,000 years old. "People told me that I'd never find anything in deep water because ancient mariners hugged the coastline," he said. "But they clung to that belief because no one had ever looked in deep water. I looked and found Roman and Phoenician boats. Ships from these times were pretty low in the water, and they didn't stand much chance in a big storm. There could be thousands down there. They went down pretty slow, and the deep seabed is soft, like a cushion, after thousands of years of slow but steady sedimentary deposits. When they sink, ships usually land upright. We could find them down there, perfectly preserved, sails still hanging from the rigging."

One year later, on May 20, 1998, Ballard discovered the *U.S.S. Yorktown*, a famous Navy ship that sank in the Pacific Ocean during World War II. This Navy ship had been sunk by a Japanese destroyer on June 7, 1942, during the Battle of Midway. But U.S. forces eventually claimed victory in the clash, and they remained in control of the region for the rest of the war.

Ballard produced both a film documentary and a book about this expedition. In both of these critically acclaimed works, the explorer combined a description of his own search with an account of the events at Midway.

Recent Expeditions

In 1999, Ballard turned his attention to the Black Sea. Some scientists had announced their belief that many years ago, melting ice caps had raised the water levels in the oceans worldwide. That, in turn, caused the Mediterranean Sea to overflow into the area of the Black Sea, which was then a freshwater lake. The overflow from the Mediterranean caused a tremendous flood, which some researchers believe may have been the famous flood associated with Noah's Ark that is described in the Bible. During the course of his exploration, Ballard gathered a variety of physical evidence that indicated that the region had indeed been the site of a great flood about 7,000 years earlier.

But Ballard's thirst for exploration is so great that he also spent some time roaming across the eastern Mediterranean Sea the same year. During this expedition, he discovered two 2,500-year old ships from the Phoenician empire sitting upright at a depth of 1,500 feet. These vessels are believed to be the two oldest shipwrecks ever found.

In 2000, Ballard and his team returned to the Black Sea. They were part of an expedition sponsored by the National Geographic Society to survey the coastal area of northern Turkey, looking for signs of human habitation about 7,000 years ago, at the time of the flood. The team found the first evidence that humans lived in the area covered by the Black Sea. About 12 miles off the coast of Turkey, in over 300 feet of water, they found a collapsed wood and clay structure. According to Ballard, "Artifacts at the site are clearly well preserved, with carved wooden beams, wooden branches, and stone tools collapsed amongst the mud matrix of the structure." Dr. Fredrik T. Hiebert of the University of Pennsylvania, the chief archeologist on the trip, was excited by the find. "This is a discovery of world importance. We have the first site with direct evidence of human occupation on the old coast. Now we can say there were people living around the Black Sea when it was a freshwater lake before it was flooded," Hiebert said. "This is a major discovery that will begin to rewrite the history of the cultures in this key area between Europe, Asia, and the ancient Middle East."

Future Plans

Ballard is currently planning a mission to locate yet another famous shipwreck. He hopes to find the final resting place of the *Endurance*, a famous ship that was crushed in the ice during Sir Ernest Shackleton's 1914 expedition to Antarctica. "*Endurance* is a great challenge," said Ballard. "You have to cut through the ice and go down 9,000 feet. I'm funded by the U.S. Navy, the National Geographic Society, and the National Oceanic and Atmospheric Administration, so I can pay to hire *HMS Endurance* [a British icebreaker] to help with the search."

But whether he finds the *Endurance* or not, Ballard insists that he will never stop his life of exploration. "The interesting thing about exploration of the sea is that it follows the classic pattern of the epic journey," he said. "You leave, go out and meet the elements — the dragon — and fight some sort of adversary. Then you attain truth, the pot of gold, and bring that back, pull up the drawbridge and lick your wounds. It's a quest." But, Ballard says, exploration is not his only goal. "The key is science. Science gives legitimacy and worth to exploration. You see a lot of stunts today but if you're not doing worthwhile science, you're not an explorer, you're just wandering around."

> ――― " ―――
>
> *Ballard says that exploration is not his only goal. "The key is science. Science gives legitimacy and worth to exploration. You see a lot of stunts today but if you're not doing worthwhile science, you're not an explorer, you're just wandering around."*
>
> ――― " ―――

MARRIAGE AND FAMILY

Ballard married Marjorie Hargas on July 1, 1966. They had two children, Todd and Douglas. Unfortunately, Todd died in a car crash in 1989, and Ballard's marriage ended in divorce in 1990. On January 12, 1991, Ballard married Barbara Earle, who had worked with him on National Geographic television specials and the JASON Project. They subsequently formed a company, Odyssey Corporation, to produce documentaries for National Geographic and others. They have two children, William and Emily, and live in Connecticut.

WRITINGS

Nonfiction

Exploring Our Living Planet, 1983
Discovery of the Titanic: Exploring the Greatest of All Lost Ships, 1987 (with Rick Archbold)
Exploring the Titanic, 1988 (juvenile)

The Discovery of the Bismarck, 1990 (with Rick Archbold)
The Lost Wreck of the Isis, 1990 (with Rick Archbold)
Exploring the Bismarck, 1991 (juvenile)
The Lost Ships of Guadalcanal, 1993 (with Rick Archbold)
Finding the Titanic, 1993 (juvenile)
Explorations: My Quest for Adventure and Discovery Under the Sea, 1995
  (with Malcolm McConnell)
*Exploring the Lusitania: Probing the Mysteries of the Sinking that Changed
  History,* 1995 (with Spencer Dunmore)
Lost Liners, 1997 (with Rick Archbold)
Ghost Liners, 1998 (with Rick Archbold)
*Return to Midway: The Quest to Find the Yorktown and the Other Lost Ships
  from the Pivotal Battle of the Pacific War,* 1999 (with Rick Archbold)
The Eternal Darkness: A Personal History of Deep-Sea Exploration, 2000 (with
  Will Hively)

Fiction

Bright Shark, 1982 (with Tony Chiu)
Ballard has also contributed dozens of articles to scientific journals and
  popular magazines.

SELECTED DOCUMENTARY FILMS

Dive to the Edge of Creation, 1980
Secrets of the Titanic, 1987
Search for Battleship Bismarck, 1989
Last Fleet of Guadalcanal, 1993
Last Voyage of the Lusitania, 1996
Battle for Midway, 1999
Lost Liners, 2000

HONORS AND AWARDS

Science Award (Underwater Society of America): 1976
Compass Distinguished Achievement Award (Marine Technology
  Society): 1977
Newcomb Cleveland Prize (American Association for the Advancement of
  Science): 1981
Cutty Sark Science Award (*Science Digest*): 1982
Secretary of the Navy Research Chair in Oceanography: 1985
Washburn Award (Boston Museum of Science): 1986

Innovations in Photography Award (American Society of Magazine
   Photographers): 1986
Centennial Award (National Geographic Society): 1988
Westinghouse Award (American Association for the Advancement of
   Science): 1990
Golden Plate Award (American Academy of Achievement): 1990
American Geological Institute Award: 1990
Computerworld Smithsonian Institution Award: 1990
Harvey Mudd College Wright Prize: 1991
Robert Dexter Conrad Award for Scientific Achievement (U.S. Navy): 1992
Hubbard Medal (National Geographic Society): 1996
International Entrepreneur of the Year: 1999
Explorer-in-Residence (National Geographic Society): 2000

FURTHER READING

Books

American Men and Women of Science, 1998
Archbold, Rick. *Deep-Sea Explorer: The Story of Robert Ballard, Discover of the
   Titanic,* 1994
Ballard, Robert, and Rick Archbold. *Discovery of the Titanic: Exploring the
   Greatest of All Lost Ships,* 1987
Ballard, Robert, and Will Hively. *The Eternal Darkness: A Personal History of
   Deep-Sea Exploration,* 2000
Ballard, Robert, and Malcolm McConnell. *Explorations: My Quest for
   Adventure and Discovery Under the Sea,* 1995
Contemporary Authors, Vol. 112, 1985
Hill, Christine M. *Robert Ballard: Oceanographer Who Discovered the Titanic,*
   1999
Polking, Kirk. *Oceanographers and Explorers of the Sea,* 1999
Something about the Author, Vol. 85, 1996
Who's Who in America, 2000

Periodicals

Boys' Life, Aug. 1994, p.28
Chicago Tribune, Mar. 19, 1987, Tempo section, p.1
Christian Science Monitor, Mar. 19, 1987, p.25
Current Biography 1986
Discover, Jan. 1987, p.50; Mar. 2000, p.110
Instructor, Mar. 1989, p.6
Los Angeles Times, Jan. 25, 1999, p.E1

National Geographic, Nov. 1989
National Geographic World, Dec. 1993, p.10
New York Times, Dec. 28, 1982, p.C1; Sep. 10, 1985, p.C3
People, Mar. 2, 1998, p.112
Readers Digest, Apr. 1992, p.173
Scholastic Update, Apr. 13, 1998, p.18
Teaching Pre K-8, Jan. 1993, p.48
Time, Aug. 11, 1986, p.48; June 26, 1989, p.46
USA Today, Mar. 1, 1999, p.D4
Washington Post, Aug. 31, 1982, p.B1; Sep. 4, 1985, p.B1; Mar. 21, 1987, p.B1

ADDRESS

Institute for Exploration
55 Coogan Boulevard
Mystic, CT 06355-1997

WORLD WIDE WEB SITES

http://www.jasonproject.org
http://www.nationalgeographic.com/blacksea/

Ben Carson 1951-

American Neurosurgeon and Author
Performed Famous 1987 Surgery to Separate
Conjoined Twins

BIRTH

Benjamin Solomon Carson was born on September 18, 1951,
in Detroit, Michigan. His parents were Robert Solomon Carson, a Baptist minister, and Sonya Copeland Carson. When
Benjamin was eight years old and his brother Curtis was ten,
their mother found out that their father had illegally married
another woman and started a second family. Sonya Carson
filed for divorce and raised her two sons as a single mother

from this time on. She supported the family by working as a domestic helper, sometimes for two or three houses at the same time.

YOUTH

Carson did not have a very happy childhood. He missed his father, and his family was very poor. "Whenever Curtis or I asked for toys or candy . . . we heard the same answer: 'We just don't have any money,'" he remembered. Sometimes he was sent to stay with relatives while his mother was treated for depression.

Carson also experienced problems with racism as a boy. He was one of only a few African-American kids in his junior high school. Once a white gang threatened to kill him if he kept going to that school. (He changed his route and never saw the gang again.) Another time, after Carson joined a neighborhood football league, he was surrounded by a group of white men after practice and warned not to come back. And when Carson won an achievement award in eighth grade, one of the teachers "bawled out the white kids because they had allowed me to be number one," he remembered. But his mother gave him good advice that helped him deal with the racism he encountered. "Always remember that if you walk into a room full of racist people, you don't have a problem, they have a problem," she told him.

Carson did not have a very happy childhood. "Whenever Curtis or I asked for toys or candy . . . we heard the same answer: 'We just don't have any money,'" he remembered.

Carson's childhood struggles made him an angry young man with a terrible temper. For many years, he fought with his brother and yelled at his mother. Once, when a friend teased him, he hit his friend in the head with a padlock, opening a large gash. Another time he broke a boy's nose by hitting it with a rock. When he was 14, he got so mad when a friend changed a station on the radio that he grabbed his camping knife and stabbed the boy in the stomach. By a miracle, the blade broke against the boy's belt buckle. The buckle protected the boy and saved Carson from possibly committing murder.

Carson credits this frightening incident with changing his attitude and behavior. "I raced to the bathroom, locked the door, and sank down on the edge of the tub," he related. He found a Bible there and started reading it.

One verse held special meaning for him: "Better a patient man than a warrior, a man who controls his temper than one who takes a city." Carson resolved then and there that with God's help he would control his temper, rather than letting his temper control him. "I can honestly say I've never been in trouble with anger since," he stated.

EDUCATION

Throughout his early school years in Detroit, where he attended Higgins Elementary and Wilson Junior High, Carson did poorly in school and was teased by his classmates. One time he got a "D" on a math test, and the teacher, trying to cheer him up, said, "Oh, Ben, you're doing so much better!" But the teacher's remark only reminded him of how badly he had been doing in his classes.

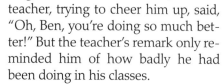

> *Carson's mother gave him good advice that helped him deal with the racism he encountered while he was growing up. "Always remember that if you walk into a room full of racist people, you don't have a problem, they have a problem," she told him.*

As it turned out, part of the reason for Carson's struggles in school was that he needed glasses and did not know it. "I thought I was too stupid to even read the letters in an eye test," he explained. "I had no idea that my eyesight had been so bad." But another problem was that he needed motivation. Luckily, his mother came through for him. First she refused to let him watch television or play after school until he learned the multiplication tables. Then she made both Benjamin and his brother read two books each week and write book reports for her. Years later they found out that, since she had only a third-grade education, she could not even read their book reports.

Sonya Carson's strategy was effective in improving her son's performance in school. One day, Carson's sixth-grade science teacher held up a rock, asking if anyone could identify it. None of the students raised their hands. Then Carson recognized it as obsidian, a type of rock that is formed when lava hits water. He had just read about it in one of his books. He raised his hand and gave the answer, surprising everyone. "You are absolutely correct," said the teacher. "If he had announced I'd won a million-dollar lottery, I couldn't have been more pleased and excited," he recalled. "It was at that moment that I realized I wasn't stupid. And I said [to myself], 'Carson, the reason you know the answer is because you've been reading those books. What if you read books in all your subjects?'" After that, there was no stopping him academically. Soon other kids began asking him to help them with their schoolwork.

By the time he entered Southwestern High School in Detroit, Carson was one of the best students in his class. He worked as a biology assistant, which increased his love of science, and he played in the band. While in high school, he also joined the Reserve Officers Training Corps (ROTC), a program that prepares students to serve as future officers in the U.S. military. His involvement in ROTC helped him avoid the pressure of having to spend money on clothes, because ROTC students wore a uniform three days each week. He graduated third in his high school class in 1969.

Carson did so well in high school that he was offered scholarships by some of the best colleges in the country, including Harvard University and Yale University. Knowing that both schools would give him an excellent education, Carson had trouble deciding between them. But one evening he watched a College Bowl program on television and saw the Yale students badly defeat the Harvard students. He ended up choosing Yale University, where he planned to study to become a doctor. "I dreamed of curing the sick, just like those missionary doctors I heard about in church," he said.

College Years

At Yale, Carson soon discovered that the science classes were much tougher than he expected. High school hadn't prepared him adequately for the intensity of the work, and he almost flunked out. His college years at Yale were the first time he was among people who were smarter than he was, and it motivated him to work even harder. "I realized I had to do a substantial rearrangement in the way I studied and become an in-depth learner," he recalls. "But I did, and rectified the problem. I just have never, under any circumstances, thought of giving up on anything I do." Carson graduated from Yale in 1973 with a bachelor's degree in psychology.

Planning to become a psychiatrist, Carson entered the University of Michigan School of Medicine. During his third year, though, he spent a month working in each of the different areas of medicine. After he had spent time in the neurosurgery department — where doctors operated on the brain, spinal cord, and other parts of the nervous system — Carson decided to become a neurosurgeon. "I loved dissecting things. And I always felt that I was very good with my hands," he said. "Neurosurgery was a natural for me." He earned his medical degree in 1977.

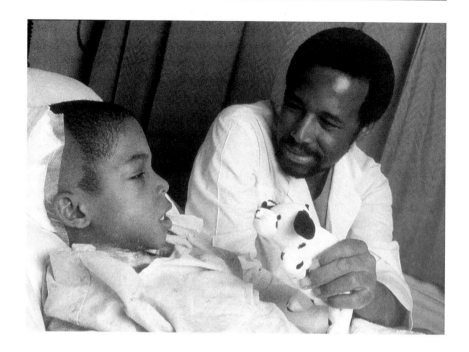

CAREER HIGHLIGHTS

After graduating from medical school, Carson's next step in becoming a doctor was to complete a training period as a resident surgeon in a hospital. He became the first African-American student to be accepted into the residency program at the Johns Hopkins University School of Medicine in Baltimore. He also spent a short time in 1981 at Baltimore City Hospital, and it was there that his surgical skills were first put to the test. Carson was on duty when a man was rushed into the emergency room. He had been badly beaten with a baseball bat and was already in a coma.

As a resident, Carson was not supposed to perform surgery without an attending surgeon present. But no senior surgeon was available, and it was clear that the man would die if he was not operated on quickly. So Carson set up an operating team and they opened the man's skull. The man's brain was already swelling, which created a dangerous situation because a swollen brain can become damaged by pressing against the skull. Carson was able to ease the swelling by cutting out parts of the brain that had already been damaged. The operation was a success, and it would be the first of many successes that soon made him famous. As a result of his outstanding performance, he won an award as Resident of the Year from Johns Hopkins in 1983.

Training in Australia

By this time, Carson had been named chief resident in neurosurgery at Johns Hopkins. But he learned that there was a severe shortage of surgeons in Australia, so he decided to complete his final year of residency at the Sir Charles Gairdner Hospital in Perth, Australia. While there, he treated a young woman who had a large tumor at the base of her skull. If left alone, the tumor would cause deafness, loss of movement of facial muscles, and finally paralysis. Carson's superiors said there was no way to remove the tumor without destroying the patient's cranial nerves, which would cause permanent brain damage. But Carson thought he could perform the surgery without damaging the nerves by using a microscopic technique. He ended up performing the surgery successfully, and the woman made a complete recovery.

Another tough case involved the fire chief in Perth. Carson discovered that the chief had an incredibly large tumor that involved all the major blood vessels in the front part of his brain. "I had to operate on the man three times to get all the tumor out," Carson remembered. Although recovery was difficult, the chief ended up doing extremely well.

By the time he had completed his year in Australia, Carson felt that he had gained more medical experience in one year than many doctors get in

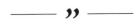

"Over time, I came to understand that the life I've had is unusual and that many people who have yet to achieve could probably identify with it. My biggest mission, I thought, was to see if perhaps something could be done, using the example of my life, to encourage others to develop a can-do — as opposed to a what-can-you-do-for-me? — attitude."

several years. All this experience gave his career a boost when he returned to Johns Hopkins in 1984. The chief of pediatric neurosurgery (a neurosurgeon who specializes in treating children) at Johns Hopkins left to take a similar job in Boston. Since Carson had so much experience and had demonstrated his skills in Australia, he was named director of pediatric neurosurgery. His area of practice involved children and young people who suffered from tumors, spasms that could not be controlled with medication, deformed spines, facial pain, and other problems relating to the brain or nervous system. There are only about 130 pediatric brain surgeons in the country.

Pioneering Work

Since taking over as chief of pediatric neurosurgery at Johns Hopkins, Carson has helped a number of challenging cases over the years. In 1985 he met Maranda, a four-year-old girl who was having as many as 120 seizures each day, sometimes only three minutes apart. During a seizure, her body would go into fits, tensing up and shaking uncontrollably. She needed to be fed through a tube so she would not choke on her food, and she needed medication all the time. The seizures were gradually damaging her brain and causing her to forget how to eat, walk, and talk. Her parents had been taking her to doctors for three years, and no one had been able to help her. They knew if her condition was not treated, she would almost certainly die.

Carson decided to perform an operation called a hemispherectomy, which is the removal of one side of the brain. It was a risky procedure, and he had never done it before. But if the operation was successful, the remaining part of the young girl's brain would take over some or all of the functions that used to be done by the other half. "We can only do this operation on young children, because their brain cells haven't decided what they want to be when they grow up," he explained. After ten hours of surgery, Maranda woke up and said, "I love you, Mommy and Daddy," despite the fact that Carson had removed the part of her brain that ordinarily controlled speech. The operation was so successful that he was invited to appear on several television shows to explain the procedure. Because of his success with this operation and many like it that followed, the hemispherectomy method is now used much more often to treat this condition.

Separating Conjoined Twins

One of Carson's most difficult surgeries involved separating a pair of twin boys, Patrick and Benjamin, who were born joined at the back of their heads. Twins who are connected at birth are known as conjoined twins (also called Siamese twins). Conjoined twins are separate people who share certain body parts. Surgery can be done to separate conjoined twins, but it is very complex. Each specific case is evaluated by a team of medical specialists. The surgery can be very risky, and it can result in the death of one or both of the twins. In the case of Patrick and Benjamin, the boys shared parts of their brains and some of the blood vessels in their heads. Siamese twins who were connected at the head had been surgically separated before, but one or both of them always died. The boys' mother did not want to sacrifice either one of her sons.

Carson decided to try a different method for this operation. He would cool the twins' blood down to 68 degrees and stop their hearts, similar to the way patients are sometimes prepared for heart surgery. Once their body functions were stopped, there would only be an hour to separate the brain matter and untangle, cut, and repair the shared blood vessels. If the operation took longer than an hour, brain damage would result. Carson assembled a team of 70 medical persons, including five neurosurgeons, two heart surgeons, five plastic surgeons, seven anesthesiologists, and many nurses and other technical assistants. He wrote ten pages of instructions and led the team through five dress rehearsals using life-size dolls.

When the actual operation began on September 5, 1987, the team ran into trouble immediately after the twins' body functions were stopped. Carson had estimated it would take only five minutes to separate the wide channels of blood surrounding the veins, but there were so many blood vessels that it took 20 minutes. This left only 40 minutes instead of 55 to rebuild the veins. Working feverishly, Carson and another surgeon finished with less than a minute to spare. "I had been holding my breath during those last few moments," remembered Carson.

The surgeons encountered another problem when the twins' hearts were started again. Rather than clotting like they were supposed to, all the tiny blood vessels in their heads kept bleeding. The situation turned into an emergency when the twins used all the available blood in the hospital. When the hospital blood bank reported that there was no more blood available in Baltimore, members of the surgical team volunteered to give their own blood. "It was a noble gesture, but not practical," recalled Carson. Fortunately, the American Red Cross came through with enough blood to last until the bleeding was controlled.

"There are opportunities everywhere," Carson says in his book THINK BIG! *"You just have to be willing to take advantage of them. Think big! Set your sights as high as Mount Everest. Nobody was born to be a failure. If you feel you're going to succeed and you work your tail off you will succeed."*

Another problem occurred a short time later when the twins' brains began to swell. They had to be put into a coma to slow their brain activity so the brains would not break through the newly repaired skulls. After 22 hours, the operation was finally completed. Years later, when the twins grew

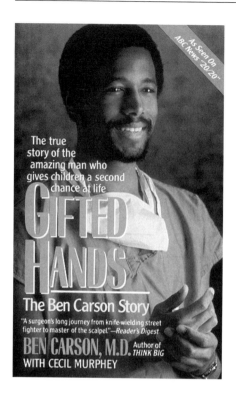

The true story of the amazing man who gives children a second chance at life

GIFTED HANDS

The Ben Carson Story

"A surgeon's long journey from knife-wielding street fighter to master of the scalpel."—*Reader's Digest*

BEN CARSON, M.D. Author of *THINK BIG*
WITH CECIL MURPHEY

older, it was discovered they had suffered some brain damage during the surgery. Still, Carson's operation was considered successful because both conjoined twins survived the delicate surgery to separate their shared brain matter.

Spreading His Formula for Success as an Author

This operation made Carson internationally famous and in great demand as a speaker. At first, he was surprised at the amount of media attention he received. But he eventually realized that people were inspired and motivated by the story of his rise to success. "Over time, I came to understand that the life I've had is unusual and that many people who have yet to achieve could probably identify with it," he noted. "My biggest mission, I thought, was to see if perhaps something could be done, using the example of my life, to encourage others to develop a can-do—as opposed to a what-can-you-do-for-me?—attitude."

To reach as many people as possible with his inspirational story and philosophy of positive thinking, Carson wrote several books. In 1990, he published his autobiography, *Gifted Hands: The Ben Carson Story.* In this book, he talks about his upbringing in a poor family and his struggles in school, and he credits his mother's influence and his faith in God for helping him find success in life. An abridged version of this book, called *Ben Carson,* was adapted for younger readers in 1992.

Also that year, Carson published a book called *THINK BIG: Unleashing Your Potential for Excellence.* In this book, he provides a series of tips to help people succeed in whatever they wish to do. The tips are outlined in the acronym THINK BIG: *T* is for recognizing and developing Talents; *H* is for living Honestly; *I* is for gaining Insight by learning from others' successes and failures; *N* is for being Nice to others; *K* is for working to increase Knowledge; *B* is for reading lots of Books; *I* is for developing In-depth knowledge in certain subjects; and *G* is for accepting the role of God in your life. "There are opportunities everywhere," he stated. "You just have to be willing to take advantage of them. Think big! Set your sights as high as Mount Everest. Nobody was born to be a failure. If you feel you're going to succeed and you work your tail off you will succeed."

In 1999, Carson published another book outlining his philosophy for success. In this book, called *The Big Picture: Getting Perspective on What's Really Important in Life*, he emphasizes that people should focus on the big picture instead of becoming bogged down in the tiny details of life. He recommends that readers ask themselves how they would like to be remembered when their lives are over in order to get a glimpse of their own priorities. The book includes many anecdotes from his medical career, as well as some of his favorite stories from the Bible. "Carson's lively storytelling will capture the hearts of his readers," wrote a reviewer for *Publishers Weekly*.

Defeats and Triumphs

In addition to his writing, Carson also continued his career as a surgeon in the 1990s. In 1993, Carson operated on Matthew, a six-year-old boy who had a tumor in his brain stem that was affecting how his eyes moved. The operation took 11 hours and appeared to be successful. Nearly two years later, though, Matthew's grandmother noticed that the boy's eyes had stopped moving normally again. An examination showed that the tumor had started growing back.

> *Carson is a devout Seventh-Day Adventist, and religion and faith in God are very important parts of his life. "God's hand is still at work in my life," he says firmly. "Do your best, and let God do the rest."*

Another operation would be necessary. This time, using a wand-like tool with special sensors at the end, Carson found the tumor buried in the scar tissue from the first surgery. Five hours later, the operation was over. Five days later, Matthew was back to a normal life. "Our hope with these kinds of tumors is that you beat them back without hurting the patient," Carson explained.

Carson attempted another separation of conjoined twins in South Africa in 1994. The fact that the location was South Africa, with its history of apartheid and racism, meant a lot to him. Unfortunately, despite the efforts of Carson and more than 24 other doctors, the operation was not a success. Both twins died. "That really took a toll on me," he admitted. Three years later, he was asked to return to South Africa to try to separate another pair of conjoined twins, who were joined at the top of the head and facing opposite directions. At first Carson hesitated. "I thought, 'Why do this again, here?'" he recalled. "But when I saw the [twins] . . . playing, so cute, I became committed to them. I thought, 'How can you not do everything to give them a normal life?'"

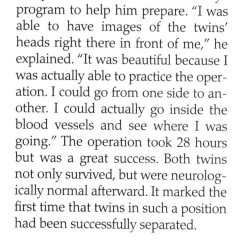

> *Carson has earned the respect and admiration of patients and fellow doctors alike. "Dr. Carson epitomizes the best that health care has to offer," said Dr. Gary C. Dennis, a former president of the National Medical Association. "He is a surgical genius and has been a role model for all youth but especially African-American youth. He has the unique balance of brilliance, commitment, and spirituality that make him a great healer for the new millennium."*

For this operation, Carson used a computer that had a "virtual reality" program to help him prepare. "I was able to have images of the twins' heads right there in front of me," he explained. "It was beautiful because I was actually able to practice the operation. I could go from one side to another. I could actually go inside the blood vessels and see where I was going." The operation took 28 hours but was a great success. Both twins not only survived, but were neurologically normal afterward. It marked the first time that twins in such a position had been successfully separated.

Recent Work

Carson added to his long list of difficult surgical procedures in 1999. His patient was 15-year-old Amber of Lincoln, Nebraska, who was having seizures nearly every hour. She suffered from a disease called Rasmussen's syndrome, in which the brain's tissue is eaten away. If not treated, Amber would become mentally retarded or paralyzed, or she would die because the diseased half of her brain would infect the good half. Carson operated for 12 hours, removing the left half of Amber's brain—the part that controls speech and small movements. When she woke up, she opened her eyes, grabbed his hand, and made sounds. "I anticipate that she will be able to speak and eventually live a quite normal life," Carson predicted.

Carson was recently featured on an ABC-TV news program performing a similar surgery. Beginning in August 2000, ABC produced a six-part series

Carson speaking to middle-school students in New Mexico, 2000.

called "Hopkins 24/7," an in-depth documentary on the successes and failures of medicine at a modern teaching hospital—Johns Hopkins. A news team spent three months filming at the hospital, with remarkable access to what went on in patients' rooms, in surgery, and in closed-door "morbidity and mortality" meetings, where doctors discuss mistakes made on patients to determine what went wrong. In one segment of the show, Carson performed a hemispherectomy, removing half of the brain of three-year old Alex, who suffered from constant seizures. The series showed Alex leaving the hospital with her parents just a week after surgery, walking and smiling.

Currently, Carson often performs as many as 12 operations each week, which adds up to 500 to 600 surgeries every year. While operating, he has classical music playing in the background, usually Bach or Schubert, "to keep me calm," he explains. His favorite part of his job is when he walks out of the operating room and says to a worried family, "Your child is awake and asking for you." "To me, that is a highlight," he says. "I love it."

Thanks to his singular accomplishments in neurosurgery, Carson has earned the respect and admiration of patients and fellow doctors alike. "Dr. Carson epitomizes the best that health care has to offer," said Dr.

Gary C. Dennis, a former president of the National Medical Association. "He is a surgical genius and has been a role model for all youth but especially African-American youth. He has the unique balance of brilliance, commitment, and spirituality that make him a great healer for the new millennium."

MARRIAGE AND FAMILY

During his junior year at Yale, Carson met his future wife, Lacena Rustin. Lacena, known as Candy, was then a new student at Yale. They were married on July 6, 1975. Candy is a classically trained musician who played first violin in the Nedlands Symphony during their year in Australia. Carson and his wife live outside Baltimore with their three teenage sons, Murray, Ben Jr., and Rhoeyce.

Carson remains close to his mother, who lives in her own wing of his home. In May 2000, Sonya Carson was honored at the Baltimore Convention Center for her determination in raising her sons and making sure they were educated against heavy odds. Carson is determined to raise his own sons with the same philosophy that helped him succeed. Using his mother's example, he limits their television viewing and requires them to read two books every week.

HOBBIES AND OTHER INTERESTS

In addition to his work as a surgeon and an author, Carson often travels to speak at schools and churches. One thing he noticed during his trips to schools was that there were many posters and trophy displays having to do with sports and entertainment. "I saw all these trophies — all-state basketball, all-state wrestling, all-state this and that," he says, "but the kids who were the academic superstars got only a National Honor Society pin and a pat on the head."

To address this situation, Carson and his wife set aside $500,000 of their own money to provide $1,000 scholarships to students who get good grades and show that they care for others. Most scholarships only give a single award, but a student can win a Carson scholarship every year from the fourth to the twelfth grade. The awards are invested and the students get financial statements every year so they can watch their savings grow. When the student is accepted into a four-year college, the scholarship money is sent to the college, and a two-and-a-half-foot trophy is sent to the student's high school for display. More than 200 schools in Delaware, Maryland, Pennsylvania, and Washington D.C. have enrolled in the program. Carson hopes to raise money and expand the program to every school in the country.

For recreation, Carson enjoys listening to classical music and playing pool and board games. He is particularly talented at the table soccer game known as Foosball. "I've never seen faster hands anywhere," says his brother Curtis. "If he has magic in his hands, it would be on a Foosball table." Carson is a devout Seventh-Day Adventist, and religion and faith in God are very important parts of his life. "God's hand is still at work in my life," he says firmly. "Do your best, and let God do the rest."

SELECTED WRITINGS

Gifted Hands: The Ben Carson Story, 1990 (with Cecil Murphy)
Ben Carson, 1992 (juvenile; with Cecil Murphy and Nathan Aaseng)
THINK BIG: Unleashing Your Potential for Excellence, 1992 (with Cecil Murphy)
The Big Picture: Getting Perspective on What's Really Important in Life, 1999 (with Gregg Lewis)

HONORS AND AWARDS

Resident-of-the-Year Award (Johns Hopkins University School of Medicine): 1983
Paul Harris Fellow (Rotary International): 1988
American Black Achievement Award (*Ebony* and Johnson Publications): 1988
Certificate of Honor for Outstanding Achievement in the Field of Medicine (National Medical Fellowship, Inc.): 1988
Candle Award for Science and Technology (Morehouse University): 1989
Blackbook Humanitarian Award (Blackbook Publishing): 1991
Horatio Alger Association Award: 1994

FURTHER READING

Books

Carson, Ben, with Cecil Murphy. *Gifted Hands: The Ben Carson Story*, 1990
Carson, Ben, with Cecil Murphy and Nathan Aaseng. *Ben Carson*, 1992 (juvenile)
Carson, Ben, with Cecil Murphy. *THINK BIG: Unleashing Your Potential for Excellence*, 1992
Contemporary Authors, Vol. 157, 1998

Kessler, James H. *Distinguished African-American Scientists of the 20th Century*, 1996
Notable Twentieth-Century Scientists, 1995
Sammons, Vivian Ovelton. *Blacks in Science and Medicine*, 1990
Simmons, Alex. *Ben Carson*, 1996
Who's Who in America, 2000

Periodicals

Baltimore Sun, Oct. 13, 1996, p.B3; Aug. 24, 1997, p.H6; May 1, 2000, p.B3
Black Enterprise, Oct. 1988, p.70
Christianity Today, May 27, 1991 p. 25
Current Biography 1997
Detroit News, Mar. 24, 2000, p.F1
Ebony, Jan. 1988, p.52
Jet, Aug. 2, 1999, p.38
New York Times, June 8, 1993, p.C1; Jan. 4, 2000, p.F7
People, June 21, 1999, p.137
Publishers Weekly, Jan. 11, 1999, p.68
Reader's Digest, Apr. 1990, p.71
Saturday Evening Post, July 1999, p.50
U.S. News & World Report, July 24, 1995, p.46
Vegetarian Times, June 1990, p.32

ADDRESS

Johns Hopkins Medical Institutions, Meyer 5-109
600 N. Wolfe
Baltimore, MD 21205

Eileen Collins 1956-

American Astronaut
First Woman to Serve as Commander of a Space
Shuttle Mission

BIRTH

Eileen Marie Collins was born on November 19, 1956, in Elmira, New York. Her father, James Collins, worked as a clerk for
the U.S. Postal Service. Her mother, Rose Marie (O'Hara)
Collins, worked as a secretary at a prison. Eileen was the second of four children born into an Irish Catholic family. She has
an older brother, a younger brother, and a younger sister.

YOUTH

"I have always had a strong desire to explore and learn. I admired pilots, astronauts, and explorers of all kinds. It was only a dream of mine that I would someday be one of them."

From the time she was a little girl, Collins was fascinated with the idea of flying. She loved to go to the local Chemung County Airport and sit on the hood of her father's car, drinking root beer and watching the planes take off and land. She also enjoyed watching gliders launch off the cliffs at nearby Harris Hill, site of the National Soaring Museum. She dreamed about exploring the skies and traveling in space. "I have always had a strong desire to explore and learn," she noted. "I admired pilots, astronauts, and explorers of all kinds. It was only a dream of mine that I would someday be one of them."

Collins's parents separated when she was nine years old, although they remained friendly and never divorced. At this time, Eileen and her siblings moved into a public housing complex with their mother. Money was tight for the family for many years. "My dad was changing jobs, and my mom was trying to get a job, so we survived on food stamps for about six months," she remembered.

Despite these hardships, Collins continued dreaming about soaring through the skies. She first became interested in space travel in the summer of 1969, when American astronauts landed on the moon for the first time. "I was 12," she recalled. "It was a Sunday night and I was camping with my family. I looked up at the moon and I was in awe of the fact that people were up there — right then. That moment reinforced my fascination with the space program." But at that point a girl could only dream. For many years, the U.S. space program only allowed male astronauts. It would be another 10 years before females were allowed into the program. In 1983, Sally Ride became the first female astronaut to fly in space.

As she grew older, Collins began reading books about flying, including military stories, space stories, and the life stories of pioneer pilots like Amelia Earhart. "When I was in my teens I started reading books on military flying — mostly about flights during World War II, and the Korean and Vietnam wars," she stated. Still, Collins never had an opportunity to fly until she traveled on a commercial jet with her mother at the age of 19. She says that she knew immediately upon taking to the air that "This is what I want to do."

EDUCATION AND MILITARY TRAINING

Collins was a solid but not exceptional student in her early school years in Elmira. Her best subject was always math. "I always did well in math," she remembered. "Back in those days—I went to school in the 1960s—girls were not encouraged to excel in math. It wasn't that we were discouraged by the teachers, but we were never really encouraged. And, of course, it was the cool thing for the boys to do well in math, but if a girl did well in math, she got picked on by the boys." Collins spent her first two years of high school at Notre Dame High, but then transferred to Elmira Free Academy for her junior and senior years. She belonged to the Spanish Club and to Future Teachers of America during her high school career. Collins graduated from Elmira Free Academy in 1974.

After finishing high school, Collins continued her studies at nearby Corning Community College. Her parents did not have the money to send her away to school, so she paid her own way with grants, loans, and part-time jobs. Collins initially planned to become a math teacher. But after she flew in an airplane for the first time, her love of flying began to affect her career plans. She became determined to take flying lessons and earn a pilot's license. She worked at a number of odd jobs in order to earn the $1,000 she needed for the lessons. For example, she was a waitress at a local pizza place, a salesperson in a catalog showroom, and a janitor in a church and a hospital. "All the money I earned from my job went to pay for my books at Corning Community College and for flying lessons," she stated. "I didn't spend money on clothes or other things."

As Collins began pursuing her dream of becoming a pilot, she did not receive much support. "When I first started taking flying lessons, people thought I was crazy," she recalled. "My friends from high school and college thought I was going off the deep end." But she continued taking the lessons for the next four years until she earned her pilot's license. She proved her natural abilities as a

"*I always did well in math. Back in those days—I went to school in the 1960s—girls were not encouraged to excel in math. It wasn't that we were discouraged by the teachers, but we were never really encouraged. And, of course, it was the cool thing for the boys to do well in math, but if a girl did well in math, she got picked on by the boys.*"

Collins at test pilot school, posing in her flight gear in front of a T-38 trainer.

pilot during her first solo flight, when the plane door popped open and she calmly continued flying. In the meantime, Collins earned an associate's degree in mathematics from Corning Community College in 1976 and went on to attend Syracuse University on a U.S. Air Force scholarship. She completed her bachelor's degree in math and economics in 1978.

Military Training

After graduating from Syracuse, Collins applied for pilot training with the Air Force. She knew it was a long shot—the Air Force had just begun accepting female pilots two years earlier—but she ended up being selected out of a group of 120 female applicants. She spent the next year at Vance Air Force Base in Oklahoma completing her undergraduate pilot training. "Acceptance into pilot training was by far the biggest break in my career," she said. "I was actually in the first class of women pilots at Vance Air Force Base. There were four of us, all 21 years old, and believe me we really stood out at a base of over 300 male pilots." Despite the high ratio of men to women, Collins did not go on a date the entire year. Instead, she chose to focus on her training. "I was not going to ruin my career by spending my time going to the movies," she explained.

"Acceptance into pilot training was by far the biggest break in my career. I was actually in the first class of women pilots at Vance Air Force Base. There were four of us, all 21 years old, and believe me we really stood out at a base of over 300 male pilots."

While Collins was in Oklahoma, the National Aeronautics and Space Administration (NASA)—which operates the American space program—began accepting female candidates for astronaut training for the first time. In fact, the first women to join the astronaut program did their parachute training at Vance Air Force Base. Seeing these women helped Collins realize that it might be possible for her to become an astronaut. "Just knowing there were women astronauts was still another milestone in my life," she stated. "That was when I first realized I wanted to be an astronaut." Collins graduated from pilot training in 1979.

Collins then remained at the base for the next three years as the first female flight instructor in the U.S. Air Force. In 1983, she transferred to Travis Air Force Base in California, where she continued to work as a flight instructor and also flew military missions. Her most important mission came in October 1983, when she flew a C-141 transport plane to the Caribbean island nation of Grenada as part of Operation Urgent Fury. In this military operation, President Ronald Reagan ordered American troops to invade Grenada and restore democratic rule after a violent overthrow of the government by Cuban-backed forces. Collins delivered 200 U.S. soldiers to

Grenada and picked up 36 American college students who were threatened by the political situation. "Of all the flights I've flown in the Air Force, that was the most rewarding because we felt like we had rescued these students, and they were so happy we had come to get them," she related.

While she was stationed in California, Collins also continued her education at Stanford University. She earned a master's degree in operations research in 1986. Later that year, she transferred to the U.S. Air Force Academy in Colorado, where she was a flight instructor and also taught math. In 1987, she married Patrick Youngs, who had been a fellow flight instructor at Travis Air Force Base. After leaving the Air Force Academy in 1989, Collins earned a second master's degree in space systems management from Webster University in St. Louis, Missouri. In 1990, she returned to California to attend Air Force Test Pilot School at Edwards Air Force Base. She was only the second woman to qualify for this top level of pilot training. More importantly for Collins, however, was the fact that military test pilot certification was a valuable asset for people hoping to become astronauts.

CAREER HIGHLIGHTS

Becoming an Astronaut

During her year of test pilot training, Collins was thrilled to learn that she had been accepted into NASA's astronaut program. By this time, she was a highly trained military pilot with the rank of lieutenant colonel. During her Air Force career, she had logged 5,000 hours in the air flying 30 different types of aircraft. Upon entering the astronaut program, Collins underwent parachute training, land and water survival training, and a period of classroom instruction about space shuttle engines, electrical systems, propulsion systems, and computers. Finally, her astronaut training also included "enrichment" courses about oceanography (scientific study of the seas), astronomy (scientific study of the stars), weather, medicine, and the history of the space program.

After successfully completing this initial training, Collins officially became a U.S. astronaut in July 1991. For the next few years, she rotated through jobs in engineering support and mission control while she learned more about the space shuttle program. NASA first began developing the space shuttle in the 1970s as a reusable vehicle to transport people and cargo to and from the earth's orbit. The first space shuttle, *Columbia,* was launched in 1981. There are now three other space shuttles in use: *Atlantis, Discovery,* and *Endeavor.* Another space shuttle, *Challenger,* tragically exploded shortly after launch in 1986.

Collins with the crew of the space shuttle Discovery *STS-63 mission, 1995.*

The space shuttle takes off from a launching pad using huge booster rockets for propulsion. Once it escapes the earth's atmosphere, the booster rockets separate from the orbiter, which carries the astronauts and cargo. The orbiter circles the earth while the astronauts deploy or retrieve satellites, conduct scientific experiments, and complete other types of missions. When this work is finished, the orbiter reenters the earth's atmosphere and lands on a runway like a commercial aircraft.

A typical space shuttle crew is led by a commander — a highly trained and experienced astronaut who actually controls the shuttle's flight and landing. The second in command is the pilot, who is trained to perform all the duties of the commander and can take over flying the shuttle as needed. The remaining crew consists of up to five mission specialists — astronauts who are responsible for space walks, scientific studies, and other specific parts of the shuttle's mission.

Thanks to her extensive training as a military pilot, Collins became the first woman in the history of the U.S. space program to qualify as a pilot on the

Collins enters notes on a log at the commander's station on Columbia's *flight deck on mission STS-93, in 1999. A small cluster of clouds can be seen out the port window.*

space shuttle. Nineteen other American women had flown in space to this point, beginning with astronaut Sally Ride in 1983, but all of these women had flown as mission specialists and scientists rather than pilots. "I'm often asked why we haven't had a woman pilot before now, and mainly the reason is we haven't had women who have had the credentials to apply to the astronaut program and compete right up there with the men," Collins explained. "We still only have a handful of women test pilots out in the military."

Before she could act as the pilot on an actual space shuttle mission, Collins had to undergo a great deal of additional training. For example, she spent up to 14 hours per day practicing takeoffs and landings in a special jet modified to fly like the space shuttle. She also spent countless hours in a machine called a simulator that was designed to function like the space shuttle in every way. "The simulator has been one of the hardest parts of my training," she admitted. "In one eight-minute ascent from launch to main engine cutoff, our trainers will input malfunctions—sometimes up to 20 different ones. You have to prioritize and organize quickly: What's wrong? How to fix? Find the procedure, then do the procedure. Then you get interrupted with another malfunction. Then you have to decide which one will 'kill me' now, in ten seconds, or minutes. . . . The reason for such intense training is that the space shuttle is really a flying computer. It has many different subsystems, which all have to be working in unison. And if something goes wrong, you need to be right on top of it."

First Woman to Pilot the Space Shuttle

In February 1995, Collins finally flew her first space shuttle mission as pilot of *Discovery.* She received a great deal of attention as the first woman pilot aboard the space shuttle. She tried to deflect some of the attention by claiming that, before long, women pilots would not be unusual. "For me, the important thing is we're going to have a second and a third and there are going to be more women and it's not going to be a big deal anymore," she stated. "It's not going to be different. It's just going to be picking the best person for the job." However, she did admit to feeling a bit of added pressure. "I can't afford to fail because I will be hurting chances for young women," she noted. "In some ways, I appreciate the stress. I want to do better and I work harder."

The *Discovery's* mission involved making a tricky approach to *Mir*, the Russian space station. *Mir* is an artificial satellite that circles the earth in a fixed orbit and serves as a base for scientific study. In future flights, American space shuttles planned to dock at *Mir* in order to transfer astronauts and supplies to the space station. *Discovery* laid the groundwork for these future flights by passing within 40 feet of *Mir* in order to test the shuttle's approach systems and communication abilities. Collins's responsibilities during the flight included steering using small rockets, and monitoring the flight instruments, radar, and navigation systems. She and the rest of the crew spent 198 hours in orbit, traveled over 2.9 million miles, and completed their mission flawlessly.

As the first woman pilot for NASA, Collins admitted to feeling a bit of added pressure. "I can't afford to fail because I will be hurting chances for young women. In some ways, I appreciate the stress. I want to do better and I work harder."

Collins enjoyed her first experience in space. Her fondest memory was watching the sun rise through the shuttle's window as they began orbiting the earth. "As I looked beyond the window, I noticed the Earth's curved horizon for the first time, with the glow and colors of the sun's rays be-

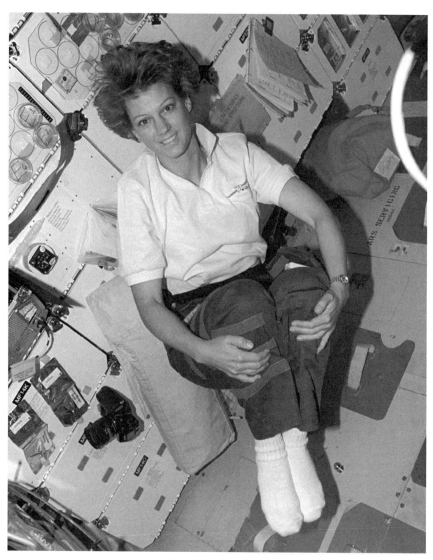

Collins floats on Columbia's *middeck during a free moment, 1999.*

yond," she recalled. "As the sun rose, it was difficult to look at, but the earth's oceans and clouds were a sight I will never forget." She also commented on the challenges of floating around in an environment without gravity. "Living and working in microgravity — or zero gravity — is very difficult at first because of the tendency to lose things, as well as the necessity to learn how to brace yourself and maneuver. But once you master these skills, life in microgravity is effortless. And fun!"

A few weeks after she returned from space, Collins learned that she was pregnant. She gave birth to a daughter, Bridget Marie, in October 1995. But Collins did not let starting a family slow her down. In May 1997, she once again served as pilot aboard the space shuttle *Atlantis*. Her mission involved docking at *Mir* for five days. During this time, the *Atlantis* crew transferred thousands of pounds of equipment and supplies to the space station, picked up American astronaut Jerry Linenger — who had been living in space for several months — and dropped off astronaut Mike Foale, and conducted a number of secondary experiments. On this flight, Collins spent 221 hours in orbit and traveled 3.8 million miles.

First Woman to Serve as Space Shuttle Commander

Under the NASA system, qualified astronauts usually fly two missions as pilot and then receive an opportunity to be commander of a space shuttle mission. In March 1998, First Lady Hillary Rodham Clinton announced that Collins had been selected as commander of the next flight of the space shuttle *Columbia*. Her selection marked the first time in 95 space shuttle missions — and 126 total American space flights — that a woman served as commander. "I'm not too concerned that I'm the first woman shuttle commander," Collins said at the time. "What's important now is that we fly a perfect mission. Whether you're commanding as a man or a woman really doesn't matter when it comes to getting the mission done."

Collins's mission, which was first scheduled for August 1998 but was delayed until July 1999, involved launching a sophisticated astronomy satellite called the Chandra X-Ray Observatory. Chandra was a huge, extremely powerful X-ray telescope that was designed to circle the earth in a high orbit and take pictures of black holes, exploding stars, and other events taking place at the edge of the universe. The observatory cost the U.S. government $2.5 billion to develop and deploy. For Collins, the most significant aspect of Chandra was that it weighed 50,000 pounds, making it the heaviest payload ever carried on a space shuttle. To complicate her mission further, *Columbia* was scheduled to make a tricky night landing for only the 12th time in shuttle history. "At night you don't have the same visual cues that you have in daytime," she explained.

But Collins was well-prepared to take command by the time *Columbia* finally launched. She flew 1,000 practice approaches and landings in the modified jet and spent countless hours in the simulator. She also worked closely with her crew and grew confident in their abilities. "As a commander, I'm big on crew resource management — the way the crew communicate with each other. Every person has a job, they do their job, but they need to be aware of what the other crew members are doing, and they need to communicate well," she noted. "I don't do everything on the shuttle. I delegate. But the commander has the ultimate responsibility for the flight, and if something goes wrong, the commander has to answer for what happened."

Collins and her crew took *Columbia* to the launching pad on July 20, but the countdown to launch was stopped with seven seconds left due to a sensor malfunction. They were all set to go again the following day, but stormy weather postponed the launch again. Collins found the delays very frustrating. "It's quite tiring," she recalled. "You get up, and you go through your briefings, you suit up, you go out to the launch pad, you climb in, you strap in, you lie on your back, in our case, for four hours while we waited for weather and/or problems to clear. And then when the scrub is called, you end up lying on your back for another hour while you reconfigure the systems to get them in a position to try the next day. And when you get out you go back to astronaut crew quarters and you desuit, and you've only got a couple of hours left in the day before you need to go to bed."

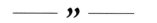

Collins's fondest memory from her first experience in space was watching the sun rise through the shuttle's window as they began orbiting the earth. "As I looked beyond the window, I noticed the Earth's curved horizon for the first time, with the glow and colors of the sun's rays beyond. As the sun rose, it was difficult to look at, but the earth's oceans and clouds were a sight I will never forget."

The space shuttle *Columbia* finally launched on July 23, 1999, with Collins making history as the first female commander in the U.S. space program. Five seconds after liftoff, however, alarms starting going off both inside the shuttle and back on earth at NASA's mission control center. It turned out that an electrical wire had short-circuited, knocking out power to the main computers controlling two of the shuttle's three engines. Luckily, the backup computers came on in time to keep the engines running and prevent Collins from having to make an unprecedented emergency landing.

A few seconds later, though, a pin came loose in one of the booster rockets and damaged the tubes carrying fuel to one of the engines. Thousands of

The five STS-93 astronauts pose for the traditional inflight crew portrait on Columbia's middeck, 1999. In front are astronauts Eileen Collins, mission commander, and Michael Tognini, mission specialist from France. Behind them are (from left) astronauts Steven Hawley, mission specialist; Jeff Ashby, pilot; and Catherine (Cady) Coleman, mission specialist.

gallons of liquid hydrogen fuel leaked out of the tank, causing the engine to shut off early. *Columbia* ended up stopping seven miles short of its target orbit height, but the crew still managed to launch the Chandra satellite and complete their mission. Collins admitted that the unexpected problems on ascent made things "interesting," but she said that her extensive training kept her from panicking. "I went right back into my simulator mode," she noted. "And I thought, 'Hey, I've been here a million times. I'll just do what I'm trained to do.' And our crew did just fantastic."

Promoting the Space Program

During her flight on board *Columbia*, Collins spent 118 hours in space and traveled 1.8 million miles. Upon returning to earth, she was invited to appear on television and radio programs across the country. She enjoyed describing the thrill of space travel to her audiences. "I'll put my face right up against a window, so I can't see anything else in the shuttle, and I'll put my arms out, and my legs out, and I feel like I'm flying over the earth with no spacecraft," she recalled. "And it's really neat. You feel like you're Superman flying over the earth."

Collins has received a number of honors since her historic flight. For example, she was inducted into the National Women's Hall of Fame, she received the State of New York's highest honor, the National Soaring Museum established an aviation summer day camp in her honor, and Corning Community College named its observatory after her. Collins took advantage of all the interviews and publicity to draw people's attention to the importance of the U.S. space program. "We need young people to pursue careers in space," she stated. "If we don't have the right people with the right know-how, we won't even be able to carry on a space program! I encourage young people to study math, science, and engineering for two reasons: to open up opportunities in technical careers and because these skills are basic in an increasingly complex world."

Here, Collins describes the thrill of space travel to her audiences. "I'll put my face right up against a window, so I can't see anything else in the shuttle, and I'll put my arms out, and my legs out, and I feel like I'm flying over the earth with no spacecraft. And it's really neat. You feel like you're Superman flying over the earth."

While Collins recognizes her own status as a pioneer among women in space travel, she often pays tribute to the many women pilots and explorers who inspired her. "I didn't get here alone. There are so many women throughout this century that have gone before me and have taken to the skies," she noted. "All these women have been my role models and inspiration and I couldn't be here today without them."

Collins is optimistic that more women will soon have a chance to follow in her footsteps. There are currently two other women astronauts who are qualified to pilot the space shuttle, Susan Still and Pam Melroy. In addition, the percentage of women among American astronauts has increased from 15 percent in 1990 to 25 percent in 1999. Finally, Collins's 1999 flight marked the 11th consecutive space shuttle mission with women on board. "It is my hope that all children, boys and girls, will see this mission and be inspired to reach for their dreams," she stated, "because dreams do come true."

Collins plans to continue her career as an astronaut and is awaiting her next assignment as commander of a space shuttle mission. "I am dedicated to maintaining the United States' leadership in space," she said. "I know how important spaceflight is to the human race overall—in technology, medicine, and economics. We can't stop exploring space, for exploring space means learning more about ourselves. I hope to continue working in these directions in whatever capacity I am needed."

MARRIAGE AND FAMILY

In 1987 Eileen Collins married Pat Youngs, a fellow Air Force flight instructor who now works as a commercial airline pilot. They have lived in Houston, Texas, since Collins became an astronaut. Their daughter, Bridget Marie, was born in October 1995, in between her mother's shuttle missions.

Collins's husband, Pat Youngs, and their daughter, Bridget, listen to members of the STS-93 crew responding to a giant welcome they received from well wishers at Johnson Space Center, 1999.

Collins admits that it is difficult being away from her daughter when she is in space, but she is able to count on her husband, a nanny, and several family members to care for Bridget. Bridget enjoys watching shuttle launches and is able to point out her mother's seat in a model space shuttle, but "I don't think she knows that everybody's mother doesn't fly in space or command a space shuttle," Collins noted.

Collins remains close to her family. "My heroes were my parents," she stated. "They've been great at motivating me and teaching me that I can become whatever I wish. I still believe in reaching one's dreams through hard work and perseverance."

HOBBIES AND OTHER INTERESTS

In her limited free time, Collins enjoys running, hiking, camping, playing golf, and reading. She also studies photography and astronomy.

HONORS AND AWARDS

Defense Superior Service Medal
Air Force Meritorious Service Medal
Air Force Commendation Medal

Armed Forces Expeditionary Medal
NASA Space Flight Medal
President's Medal (New York Institute of Technology): 1996
National Women's Hall of Fame: 1998
Humanitarian Award (Ernie Davis Heisman Memorial Fund): 2000
Legion of Honor (France): 2000

FURTHER READING

Books

Encyclopedia of World Biography, 1998
Haynsworth, Leslie, and David Toomey. *Amelia Earhart's Daughters,* 1998
Notable Women Scientists, 2000
Who's Who in America, 2000

Periodicals

Los Angeles Times, Nov. 24, 1991, p.B6
Ms., July/Aug. 1998, p.23
New York Times, Feb. 1, 1995, p.A22; Feb. 6, 1995, p.B1
Orlando Sentinel, Jan. 29, 1995, p.A1; July 18, 1999, p.A14; July 28, 1999, p.A1
People, May 11, 1998, p.225
Seventeen, Nov. 1999, p.80
Sky and Telescope, Oct. 1999, p.16
Spaceflight, Dec. 1999, p.517
Time for Kids, Mar. 13, 1998, p.3
USA Today, July 16, 1999, p.A7; July 19, 1999, p.A17
Washington Post, Feb. 4, 1995, p.A3

ADDRESS

NASA
Lyndon B. Johnson Space Center
Houston, TX 77058

WORLD WIDE WEB SITES

http://www.jsc.nasa.gov/bios/htmlbios/collins.html
http://www.health.org
http://quest.arc.nasa.gov
http://starchild.gsfc.nasa.gov

Biruté Galdikas 1946-

German-Born Canadian Primatologist
Leading Researcher on Behavior of Endangered
Indonesian Orangutans
Established Orangutan Foundation International to
Protect Orangutans and Their Habitat

BIRTH

Biruté Galdikas (pronounced bi-ROO-tay GALD-i-kus) was
born in Wiesbaden, West Germany, on May 10, 1946, to Anatanas and Filomena Galdikas. Two years later, the Galdikas
family emigrated from Europe to Canada. The family soon set-

tled in Toronto, Ontario, where Anatanas worked as a miner, machinist, and painting contractor and Filomena found employment as a nurse. Biruté is the oldest of their four children. She has two younger brothers, Vytas and Al, and one younger sister, Aldona.

YOUTH

Biruté Galdikas's lifelong interest in exploration and seeking out new experiences began in her early childhood, when she experimented with all sorts of activities. For example, she took violin, piano, and ballet lessons, and harbored dreams of someday growing up to be a ballerina. In addition, she developed a deep interest in reading at an early age. The very first book that she borrowed from the library was *Curious George,* a famous children's book about a friendly monkey and his adventures. Before long, she was spending hours at the Toronto Public Library, reading more challenging books about science, natural history, and the world of animals.

> "On weekends my family picnicked in parks and yards near downtown Toronto, or went hiking, camping, and fishing in the vast forests of northern Ontario. Because of my parents' fondness for nature, I became that unlikely combination of bookworm and nature lover. . . . In grade two, I had decided on my life's work; I wanted to be an explorer."

As Galdikas grew older, she developed a fascination with the outdoors that remained with her for the rest of her life. She often roamed through the streams and woods of local parks, studying plants and trees and observing salamanders, ducks, and turtles. She also loved to stroll through the city zoo and watch the fascinating creatures that lived there. In addition, she spent many childhood weekends at a remote cabin that was owned by the family of a childhood friend. On these summer weekends, Galdikas and her friend would spend hours fishing, hiking, and exploring the deep green woods that surrounded the cabin.

Galdikas's parents also helped nurture her appreciation for the natural world, in part because they enjoyed the outdoors so much themselves. "On weekends my family picnicked in parks and yards near downtown Toronto, or went hiking, camping, and fishing in the vast forests of northern Ontario," Galdikas later recalled. "Because of my parents' fondness for nature, I became that unlikely combination of bookworm and nature lover. . . . In grade two, I had decided on my life's work; I wanted to be an explorer."

EDUCATION

Both of Galdikas's parents were originally from Lithuania, a country in northeastern Europe, and they usually spoke Lithuanian to each other and their children around the house. As a result, the first language that Galdikas learned was Lithuanian. In fact, on her first day of kindergarten in Toronto, she could not understand her teacher or her fellow students because they were all speaking English. Within a year, though, she had learned English and become thoroughly bilingual.

Galdikas attended public schools in the Toronto area until 1962, when her family moved to Vancouver, British Columbia, the westernmost province in Canada. There, she earned excellent grades throughout elementary and high school. Her academic performance greatly pleased her parents, who believed that knowledge and education would be vital to her future success and happiness. "My parents stated clearly that because we were 'New Canadians' and had no family connections in Canada, the only way that we children could get ahead was through education," Galdikas recalled in her autobiography, *Reflections of Eden*. "I was the oldest child, and my mother believed that my education came before all else."

Attending College in the United States

After a short stay in Vancouver, the Galdikas family moved on to southern California. In 1965 Galdikas enrolled in the University of California at Los Angeles (UCLA), which seemed to her to be the most exciting and vibrant place in the world. Determined to make the most of her college experience, she became a whirlwind of activity. "I took a variety of undergraduate courses at UCLA, ranging from invertebrate marine biology to industrial psychology," she said. "I raced from class to class, studied with my friends, spent hours in the library, went to film festivals and rock concerts, carpooled, and went to the beach."

As her college education progressed, Galdikas eventually decided to pursue a bachelor's degree in anthropology, the study of the physical and cultural development of mankind through history. She later admitted, though, that as she worked toward her degree, she could not help feeling like she was getting away with something. "Taking anthropology as a major seemed like a sin," she explained. "I liked it too much. I didn't want

to waste my tuition money to pay for something I enjoyed so much." In 1966 Galdikas graduated with honors. But she decided to continue her education, setting her sights on earning a master's degree in anthropology.

As Galdikas continued her studies of human evolution and social development at UCLA, she felt increasingly intrigued by the world's ape species. Apes — chimpanzees, gorillas, and orangutans — are members of the same biological family as humans. As such, apes are humankind's closest living relatives. Galdikas felt particularly drawn to orangutans, the most mysterious of the great apes. She realized that far less was known about the lives of these creatures than about either chimpanzees or gorillas, and an overwhelming curiosity about orangutan life began to sweep over her. Over the course of several months, she decided that she wanted to initiate the first major study of orangutans in Indonesia, the only place on earth where wild orangutans still lived.

"My vision of studying orangutans became stronger with time," Galdikas recalled in her autobiography. "My obsession with the rare red ape increased. I spoke to some of my professors at UCLA about a wild orangutan study, but they were quietly discouraging. A few said bluntly that such a study simply couldn't be done. If I couldn't get academic support for a study of wild orangutans, I decided, I would finish my doctorate, save my money, and go to the forests of Southeast Asia independently. It was simply what I felt I must do, a personal quest."

> While in college, Galdikas decided that she wanted to initiate a study of orangutans in the wild in Indonesia. "I spoke to some of my professors at UCLA about a wild orangutan study, but they were quietly discouraging. A few said bluntly that such a study simply couldn't be done. If I couldn't get academic support for a study of wild orangutans, I decided, I would finish my doctorate, save my money, and go to the forests of Southeast Asia independently. It was simply what I felt I must do, a personal quest."

Seeking Sponsorship from Louis Leakey

In 1969 Galdikas attended a lecture at UCLA given by Louis Leakey, the famous paleontologist (a scientist who studies fossils). During the 1940s and 1950s, Louis Leakey and his wife, Mary Leakey, had discovered thousands of ancient fossils in East Africa that changed many scientific theories of human evolution. Then, in the 1960s, he had helped launch important research work that increased understanding of the lives of both chimpanzees and gorillas. In fact, he had emerged as a major sponsor of both Jane Goodall, who led landmark field studies on chimpanzees, and Dian Fossey, who led similar studies on mountain gorillas. (For further information on Louis and Mary Leakey, Jane Goodall, and Dian Fossey, see the entries in *Biography Today Scientists & Inventors,* Vol. 1.)

Leakey's fame and reputation for brilliance was very intimidating. But as Galdikas listened to him speak, she realized that he might be able to help her realize her dream of undertaking a major study of orangutan life. With this in mind, she boldly approached the paleontologist as soon as he concluded his talk. "After the lecture I told him I wanted to study orangutans," she recalled. "He said he was going back to Africa the next day but would keep in touch. I walked out of that hall convinced I was going to study orangutans. . . . Leakey didn't care about formal education. He wanted enthusiasm, belief in what you were doing."

Over the next several months, Leakey and Galdikas continued to talk about her research proposal. He gradually became convinced of her dedication to the project and agreed to sponsor her. Galdikas then spent the next two years dividing her time between planning the project and continuing her studies. By mid-1971, she and Leakey had finally raised enough money for her to go to Indonesia, home of the mysterious orangutan. Several years later, Galdikas completed her Ph.D. in anthropology at UCLA in 1978.

CAREER HIGHLIGHTS

Arriving in Borneo

In September 1971, Galdikas departed for Indonesia with her husband, Rod Brindamour, whom she had married in 1969. The adventurous Brindamour shared his wife's excitement about the orangutan study. He agreed to go to Indonesia in order to help establish a work site and photograph the project's development. But as Galdikas later admitted, Brindamour never intended to spend the rest of his life in Indonesia. "I planned to go to the wilds of Borneo and Sumatra, and Rod wanted to see the world," she said in *Reflections of Eden.* "Somewhere along the line I guess I should have told him that I wasn't coming back."

Upon arriving in Indonesia, Galdikas met with national forestry officials. They arranged for her to base her study in Tanjung Puting Reserve, a remote jungle area of Borneo that seemed to support a healthy population of orangutans. She and her husband then packed backpacks, clothing, photographic equipment, food, books and magazines, and assorted other items onto big dugout canoes that would take them to their new home.

Galdikas's son, Binti, with a baby orangutan.

On November 6, 1971, the couple completed their journey into Tanjung Puting Reserve. They floated their canoes down the Sikunir Kanan River until they reached a small clearing with an abandoned logger's hut. It was here that they began the process of building a home for themselves. All around them was a 1,200-square-mile mix of swamp and rainforest that

———— " ————

When she and her husband settled in Indonesia, according to Galdikas, "the true hazards of the rainforest were little nagging things like viruses, parasites, insects, and plant toxins. The leeches were so abundant that we lost track of how many we took off our bodies during the course of any one day. Bloated with our blood, leeches fell out of our socks, dropped off our necks, and squirmed out of our underwear."

———— " ————

hid everything from king cobras to vicious wild pigs. But according to Galdikas, "the true hazards of the rainforest were little nagging things like viruses, parasites, insects, and plant toxins. The leeches were so abundant that we lost track of how many we took off our bodies during the course of any one day. Bloated with our blood, leeches fell out of our socks, dropped off our necks, and squirmed out of our underwear."

Weather conditions also made it difficult for Galdikas and Brindamour to get comfortable. The rainforest was so humid and wet that their clothes seemed perpetually damp and their books became soggy and mildewed. But despite the uncomfortable environment, the couple slowly built a life for themselves out in the remote jungle. Brindamour built a new cabin out of ironwood, a kind of wood that was highly resistant to the damp climate, and hacked a system of trails deep into the jungle. When the camp was completed, they named it Camp Leakey in honor of their sponsor. Galdikas, meanwhile, began venturing deep into the rainforest in search of orangutans. "I'd just take a jar full of cold coffee and go from early morning to late in the afternoon, [often wading] up to my armpits in water," she recalled.

Searching for the Mysterious Orangutan

"When I went into the field, virtually nothing was known about the life of orangutans in the wild," Galdikas stated in *Reflections of Eden*. "Several researchers had conducted one- or two-year field studies. But the terrain in Borneo and Sumatra is difficult, and orangutans, living high in the forest canopy, are elusive. These researchers had not been able to habituate the red apes or to follow the same individuals for any length of time. Science had 'snapshots,' but little information on orangutan life histories or orangutan social organization."

The lack of scientific knowledge about orangutans was due in part to the secretive and solitary nature of these apes. "In social behavior the orangutan has always been considered very different not only from man but also from all other monkeys and apes, including its African cousins, the gorilla and chimpanzee," confirmed Galdikas. But the shortage of information also was attributed to their diminishing population. Orangutans are an endangered species, with an estimated population of only 20,000-30,000 left in the world. "Rarest of the apes, wild orangutans are restricted to diminishing ranges on the islands of Borneo and Sumatra," she explained. "It has long been illegal in Indonesia and Malaysia to own, kill, or export them, but until recently the laws were not strictly enforced. The threat of extinction still hangs over the orangutan because of the slaughter of mothers by poachers trying to capture their infants [to sell to zoos and people who keep them as exotic pets] and the wholesale destruction of their habitat by logging and agricultural land-clearing operations." Galdikas hoped that she could break through the veil of mystery that surrounded the ape before the last pockets of orangutan habitat vanished forever.

Studying the Red Ape

Galdikas's exhausting tramps into the jungle often ended in disappointment. On most days, she pushed deep into the rainforest in search of orangutans, only to return to Camp Leakey with nothing to show for her efforts. Gradually, however, she developed a talent for spotting the apes. "My earliest observations were of orangutans feeding, moving through the trees, and nesting," she recalled. "My first years in the field were years of discovery, when merely finding a wild orangutan was exciting, when following an orangutan for a week or more was a triumph, when almost everything I learned about orangutans was new." After a while, she became so familiar with nearby orangutans that she learned to recognize individual apes by the size and shape of their face, scars, missing fingers, and other distinguishing features.

As the months and years passed by, Galdikas made many important discoveries about orangutan behavior. For example, she learned a great deal about their dietary habits and their verbal and nonverbal methods of communicating. She also documented orangutan mating habits and reproductive cycles, and became the first person to witness the birth of a wild orangutan. In addition, her studies proved that wild orangutans sometimes used tools (like sticks) and occasionally ate meat. Finally, she learned that orangutans had a very highly developed social structure. "Orangutans have the most intense mother-child relationship of any primate with the exception of humans," Galdikas has stated. All of these discoveries increased her admiration and passion for the tree-dwelling apes. "For the first ten years I was here [at Camp Leakey], I wanted to be an orangutan," she later said.

In the early 1970s, Galdikas and Brindamour converted their camp in Tanjung Puting Reserve into an orangutan rehabilitation center. They used the facility to care for young orangutans who had been orphaned or raised in captivity. They raised some orphaned apes for as long as eight years, the length of time an orang mother would normally spend raising her child. Galdikas's ultimate goal, however, was to gradually prepare the orangutans to support themselves in the wild.

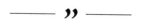

"My earliest observations were of orangutans feeding, moving through the trees, and nesting," she recalled. "My first years in the field were years of discovery, when merely finding a wild orangutan was exciting, when following an orangutan for a week or more was a triumph, when almost everything I learned about orangutans was new."

Caring for Baby Orangutans

As the number of orphaned orangutans at Camp Leakey continued to grow, it became a real challenge to provide for all their needs. Galdikas and Brindamour had to attend to the young apes' medical and nutritional requirements, as well as their emotional needs. "[They] were insatiably curious, wanted constant affection and attention, [and] expressed emotions such as anger and embarrassment in a manner seemingly very similar to human beings," Galdikas remarked.

At times, the environment at Camp Leakey seemed to veer toward the edge of chaos, despite the fact that Galdikas added Indonesian staff to help care for the apes and assist in her research. "Sometimes I felt as though I were surrounded by wild, unruly children in orange suits who had not yet learned their manners," she recalled. "There was nothing in our hut . . . that had not been tasted, chewed, or at least mouthed by an orangutan. Everything had orangutan tooth marks on it. Nothing was immune. For nesting material, the curious youngsters ripped apart our clothes, our books, and even our umbrella. They carried our mosquito net into the trees, ate our candles, chewed on the binoculars, tasted batteries, and drank our shampoo. They found tubes of toothpaste and glue irresistible, and opening our purportedly fail-safe,

toddler-proof medicine bottles was child's play for the animals. . . . It was a continual battle of wits, and they won!"

But despite the exasperation and anger that she sometimes felt when caring for these rambunctious young apes, Galdikas found raising the orangutan orphans to be an intensely rewarding experience. "Most [orphan orangutans] arrive worm-infested, stunted, diseased," wrote Sy Montgomery in

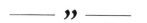

"Sometimes I felt as though I were surrounded by wild, unruly children in orange suits who had not yet learned their manners," Galdikas said about the orphaned baby orangutans at her camp. "There was nothing in our hut . . . that had not been tasted, chewed, or at least mouthed by an orangutan. Everything had orangutan tooth marks on it. Nothing was immune. . . ."

Walking with the Great Apes. "Many have died in [Galdikas's] arms. But those who survive their infancy are then free . . . to roam through camp and its outlying forests until they voluntarily leave for life in the wild." To Galdikas, these success stories made all the other inconveniences of her life worthwhile.

A Time of Triumph and Heartache

During the late 1970s, Galdikas became known as one of the world's leading authorities on orangutans. In 1978 she completed a Ph.D. dissertation on orangutan behavior that was widely praised for increasing human understanding of the species. She also wrote about her experiences with orangutans in *National Geographic*, and her lengthy cover stories for the magazine in October 1975 and June 1980 brought her widespread attention. In addition, she supervised the expansion of Camp Leakey from a single cabin to a compound of eight buildings that housed local staff, members of the Indonesian Forestry Department, and college students from Indonesian and North American colleges. By 1979, Galdikas estimated that she and her staff had amassed more than 12,000 hours of observation of the endangered apes.

Galdikas and Brindamour also started a family during this period. In 1976 Galdikas gave birth to a boy they called Binti. He was a strong, healthy child, and at first they tried to raise him at Camp Leakey. But as Binti grew older, his parents saw that the boy's constant exposure to orphan orangutans was having a negative impact on his development. "When I carried him, he would often dangle his arms in the loose manner of an orangutan," Galdikas recalled. "In fact, at the age of three he could do a perfect orangutan imitation. It would not have been any cause for concern except that, with no other children in camp, orangutans were becoming his role models."

Meanwhile, Galdikas's marriage to Brindamour began to crumble. Galdikas loved her research work in the rainforest and did not want to leave Borneo. But Brindamour was weary of living in the jungle, and he wanted to pursue a career in computer science. He also believed that long-term use of an antimalarial drug was causing damage to his eyes. Finally, he had fallen in love with Binti's nanny, a young Indonesian woman named Yuni.

In mid-1979 Brindamour and Yuni left Indonesia for Canada, where they intended to build a new life for themselves. Several months later, Galdikas reluctantly admitted that Binti needed to grow up with other children. "Six months after Rod left, I took Binti to North America to enter nursery school," she remembered. "It was the most difficult decision I ever made. But I felt strongly that Binti should be educated in North America and that a boy should live with his father." During this trip, Galdikas finalized her divorce and accepted a part-time faculty position in the Department of Archaeology at Simon Fraser University in British Columbia. This appointment meant that she would at least be able to see Binti for a few months each year.

After returning to Borneo, Galdikas helped lead a campaign to convince the Indonesian government to make the Tanjung Puting preserve a national park. In fact, Galdikas made major contributions to the management plan for the proposed park. She and other supporters of the proposed park knew that if the government approved the plan, the orangutans' rainforest home would receive much greater protection from illegal logging, poaching, and other activities that threatened the region and its wildlife. In 1982, the efforts of Galdikas and her allies paid off, as Indonesian authorities formally gave national park status to the Tanjung Puting region.

". . . For nesting material, the curious youngsters ripped apart our clothes, our books, and even our umbrella. They carried our mosquito net into the trees, ate our candles, chewed on the binoculars, tasted batteries, and drank our shampoo. They found tubes of toothpaste and glue irresistible, and opening our purportedly fail-safe, toddler-proof medicine bottles was child's play for the animals. . . . It was a continual battle of wits, and they won!"

Advocate for Orangutans

Galdikas viewed the creation of Tanjung Puting National Park as a great triumph. But she recognized that other threats to the orangutan's long-term survival remained. For example, many wealthy and powerful Indonesians viewed orangutan ownership as a symbol of prestige. But Galdikas

Binti and Galdikas in 1980.

knew that many of these orangutans had been seized from the wild by poachers who did not think twice about killing mother orangs in order to grab their babies. She subsequently launched a quiet but determined campaign to teach Indonesians about this horrible practice and dissuade them from keeping orangutans as pets.

Galdikas's education campaign, which began in the mid-1970s and intensified during the 1980s, helped bring about a dramatic change in the way that Indonesians saw orangutan ownership. Seizures of the apes from the wild dropped dramatically, and many people agreed to give their pet orangs to Galdikas's facility or other rehabilitation centers so that they could eventually be trained to return to the rainforest. Galdikas attributed the success of this campaign to her ability to raise her concerns without angering the Indonesian government or its people. "If there's a problem [in Indonesian society], you can't just rush in and solve it," she explained. "You establish that you're not going to make troubles. I am careful about what I ask for. I don't impose myself on them. My gut feeling is that when I walk through somebody's door, they don't say, 'Ah, here comes a problem.' They say, 'Ah, here comes my friend.'"

In 1987 Galdikas's continuing interest in orangutan welfare led her to establish an organization called Orangutan Foundation International (OFI) that works on behalf of both wild and captive orangutans in Indonesia and around the world. Many environmentalists praised the creation of Orangutan Foundation International and expressed support for its mission. But some primatologists (people who engage in the scientific study of apes) viewed the creation of OFI as the final stage in Galdikas's gradual transition from scientist to wildlife advocate.

Dogged by Controversy

During the first two decades that Galdikas spent in Borneo, she was hailed for her work as both a scientist and a defender of wildlife. In recent years, however, her activities and operations have become the subject of considerable controversy.

Questions about Galdikas's OFI organization first erupted in 1990, when it became involved in two strange orangutan smuggling cases. In the first of these cases, six baby orangutans who had been secretly taken out of Borneo were discovered at a Thailand airport. The "Bangkok Six," as the orangutans came to be known, were given to Galdikas to nurse back to health. But several of the baby orangutans subsequently died in the care of OFI. Then, eight months later, the government of Taiwan arranged to return ten stolen orangutans to Borneo. At first, these orangutans — known as the "Taiwan Ten" — were placed in the care of Galdikas and her staff. But a mysterious tug of war for control of the apes soon exploded.

As her son was growing up in the wild, Galdikas felt that the boy's constant exposure to orphan orangutans was having a negative impact on his development. "When I carried him, he would often dangle his arms in the loose manner of an orangutan. In fact, at the age of three he could do a perfect orangutan imitation. It would not have been any cause for concern except that, with no other children in camp, orangutans were becoming his role models."

After more than a year of squabbling, Indonesian authorities seized the apes from Galdikas and transferred them to other orangutan rehabilitation centers around the country.

In the months following these two incidents, some observers suggested that Galdikas's efforts on behalf of orangutans were not as effective as they had been in the past. Others speculated that her relations with

Indonesian authorities and communities had become strained over the years. But many supporters came to her defense. "Nobody's been with orangutans as long as she has or knows as much about them," said a member of Orangutan Foundation International in 1992. "To do what she does takes tremendous grit and a willingness to put up with not just the uncomfortable aspects of living out in the tropics but the politics and logistics of it all. That's the whole reason there aren't more people doing these kinds of studies. It's extremely difficult to keep up that energy level, and she's done it."

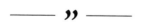

"We tend to think that the other creatures who share our planet inhabit the same reality as we do, especially if they resemble us, as monkeys and apes do. But their senses, their needs, their perceptions are not the same as ours. Communing with a wild animal of another species means glimpsing another reality."

In the mid-1990s, Galdikas published two books about the orangutans of Borneo. In the first of these, a 1995 autobiography called *Reflections of Eden: My Years with the Orangutans of Borneo,* Galdikas discussed her experiences in the rainforest and tried to explain her continued fascination with the red apes who inhabit the region. "We tend to think that the other creatures who share our planet inhabit the same reality as we do, especially if they resemble us, as monkeys and apes do," she wrote. "But their senses, their needs, their perceptions are not the same as ours. Communing with a wild animal of another species means glimpsing another reality."

Reflections of Eden was warmly received by reviewers and conservationists alike. A review in *The New Yorker* called the book "enthralling" and stated that "her beautifully written account shows both the pleasures and the value of making a connection with another species." Fellow primatologist Jane Goodall, meanwhile, called the autobiography "an unforgettable book written by a remarkable woman."

In 1999 Galdikas collaborated with Nancy Briggs to write a second book about the orangutans of Borneo, called *Orangutan Odyssey.* This book, which describes orangutan behavior and threats to their future, included dozens of dazzling color photographs of the apes in their native habitat. *Publishers Weekly* called it a "memorable, informal, and attractive" work.

Accusations of Mistreatment

But complaints about Galdikas's operations in Borneo also increased in the mid-1990s. During that time, some observers charged that she exercised too much control over the lives of staff and volunteers at OFI and the Tanjung Puting facility. This claim was hotly denied, though, by Galdikas, OFI spokespersons, and several staff members and volunteers.

A more serious charge was leveled against Galdikas in 1997. At that time, several former volunteers who had worked for her alleged that she was illegally keeping orangutans at a house in Pasir Panjang, where she had taken up part-time residence. These volunteers claimed that nearly 100 orangutans—many of them abducted from the national park— were being kept in cages behind her house. These witnesses claimed

Galdikas holding hands with a playful orangutan, 1997.

that the orangutans were held in filthy and overcrowded conditions and that their basic medical and nutritional needs were not met. Their accounts described sick orangutans lying untended in pools of diarrhea and untrained keepers who sometimes blew smoke in the animals' faces. Finally, these witnesses charged that as many as 21 orangutans had died at Galdikas's house because of insufficient care or medical mistreatment.

These charges triggered an official government investigation. In March 1998 government investigators went to the Galdikas house in Pasir Panjang. According to their report, they found 89 orangutans hidden in "four secret lodges placed in the forest behind the house." They also learned that Galdikas had nearly completed construction of an "Orang-utan Care and Quarantine Center" at the home without first securing government approval. Indonesian officials immediately ordered her to stop construction of the center.

One year later, a writer named Linda Spalding published a highly critical article in *Outside* magazine that examined Galdikas's operations in Borneo.

In the article — and in a book called *A Dark Place in the Jungle,* published in 1999 — Spalding claimed that Galdikas was a rude and domineering figure who no longer engaged in any meaningful orangutan research. For example, the author revealed that Galdikas had lost her permit to continue research work at Camp Leakey back in 1993 because she refused to submit reports to the authorities on her research or the status of the orangutan population. This setback apparently convinced Galdikas to move her orangutan operations to her home in Pasir Panjang, although she continued to visit the national park on a regular basis.

>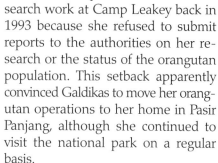
>
> *Galdikas continues to fight excessive mining and logging practices that threaten the orangutan's home in the rainforests of Borneo.*
> *"If we can employ villagers who are illegally mining and cutting forests, we may be able to slow the rate of destruction to the rainforest, which is the life system of the orangutan,"she said. But Galdikas confessed that the future of the orangutan remained in doubt.*
> *"They are poised on the edge of extinction,"she warned.*
> *"It's that simple."*

Spalding also suggested that Galdikas might actually be hurting the cause of Indonesia's orangutan population. In order to support this claim, she quoted several observers who harshly criticized Galdikas's actions in recent years. "She began as a scientist," charged Earthwatch Europe deputy director Andrew Mitchell in *Outside,* "but she has become more and more attached to the animals and more and more involved in conflicts with local people and the authorities. I fear that she is shipwrecking herself."

Galdikas and her many supporters angrily denied these charges, however. They claimed that orangutans under her care were well-treated and that she remained committed to her research work. In July 1999 Galdikas filed a lawsuit against Spalding, claiming that her article and book included false statements that damaged her reputation and resulted in the loss of research funding.

Continuing Efforts to Protect Orangutans

In 1999 Galdikas declared that despite conservation efforts of the previous two decades, Indonesia's orangutans continued to be threatened by excessive logging and mining practices. "We're doing what we can," she said. "We're trying to set up patrols of local men to go out with park rangers so that when they come across illegal loggers, they don't feel totally intimidated. We're working with the Indonesian government to set up new wildlife reserves at expired logging concessions. And of course, we're doing what we always have: saving wild-born orangutans who've been captured by humans."

In the spring of 2000 Galdikas announced a $10 million fund-raising drive to keep the people of Borneo from destroying the remaining sections of rainforest. "If we can employ villagers who are illegally mining and cutting forests, we may be able to slow the rate of destruction to the rainforest, which is the life system of the orangutan," she said. But she confessed that the future of the orangutan remained in doubt. "They are poised on the edge of extinction," she warned. "It's that simple."

MARRIAGE AND FAMILY

Galdikas married Rod Brindamour in 1969. Their marriage ended in 1979, when Brindamour left the jungle. They had one child, Binti—which means "small bird" in a local Indonesian language—who was born in 1976.

In 1981 Galdikas remarried. Her second husband is Pak Bohap bin Jalan, a member of a native Borneo tribe known as the Dayak. They have two children, Frederick and Jane (named after Galdikas's good friend Jane Goodall).

HOBBIES AND OTHER INTERESTS

Galdikas spends most of her time engaged in orangutan preservation and research issues. But she also likes to read and study Indonesian culture.

WRITINGS

Books

Reflections of Eden: My Years with the Orangutans of Borneo, 1995
Orangutan Odyssey, 1999 (with Nancy Briggs)

Periodicals

"Orangutans, Indonesia's 'People of the Forest,'" *National Geographic,* Oct. 1975
"Living with the Great Orange Apes," *National Geographic,* June 1980
"My Life with Orangutans," *International Wildlife,* Mar./Apr. 1990

HONORS AND AWARDS

PETA Humanitarian Award (People for the Ethical Treatment of Animals): 1990
Chico Mendes Conservation Award (Sierra Club): 1992
United Nations Global 500 Environment Award (United Nations): 1993
Officer of the Order of Canada: 1995
Tyler Prize for Environmental Achievement: 1997

FURTHER READING

Books

Facklam, Margery. *Wild Animals, Gentle Women,* 1978 (juvenile)
Galdikas, Biruté. *Reflections of Eden: My Years with the Orangutans of Borneo,* 1995
Gallardo, Evelyn. *Among the Orangutans: The Birute Galdikas Story,* 1993 (juvenile)
Kevles, Bettyann. *Watching the Wild Apes,* 1976 (juvenile)
Montgomery, Sy. *Walking with the Great Apes: Jane Goodall, Dian Fossey, Birute Galdikas,* 1991
Spalding, Linda. *A Dark Place in the Jungle: Scientists, Orangutans, and Human Nature,* 1999
Who's Who, 1999
Yount, Lisa. *A to Z of Women in Science and Math,* 1999
Yount, Lisa. *Twentieth-Century Women Scientists,* 1996

Periodicals

Christian Science Monitor, Jan. 13, 1992, p.14
Current Biography 1995
Highlights for Children, Sep. 1998, p.8
International Wildlife, Mar.-Apr. 1990, p.34
Interview, Mar. 1995, p.100
Life, Aug. 1990, p.70; May 1998, p.66
Los Angeles Times, Jan. 19, 1997, p.L8
National Geographic, Oct. 1975, p.444; June 1980, p.830
National Geographic World, Apr. 1994, p.10
New York Times, May 1, 1981, p.B4; Aug. 16, 1992, section 6, p.29; Mar. 21, 2000, p.D3
New York Times Magazine, Aug. 16, 1992, p.29
Newsweek, June 1, 1998, p.58
Omni, July 1987, p.76

Outside, May 1998, p.58
People, Jan. 16, 1989, p.102
Saturday Night, Jan. 1988, p.46
Science, Apr. 16, 1993, p.420
Washington Post, May 1, 1981, p.D1

Documentary Films

The Third Angel, 1991
In the Wild, 1998

ADDRESS

Orangutan Foundation International
822 South Wellesley Avenue
Los Angeles, CA 90049

WORLD WIDE WEB SITES

http://www.science.ca/scientists/Galdikas
http://www.orangutan.org

Lonnie Johnson 1949-

American Engineer and Businessman
Inventor of the Super Soaker

BIRTH

Lonnie G. Johnson was born in 1949 in Mobile, Alabama.
Little information is available about his family background.

YOUTH AND EDUCATION

As a boy, Johnson enjoyed taking things apart to see how
they worked. He often tried to use what he learned to invent

something new. One day he tried to make some rocket fuel, but he only succeeded in starting a fire. In high school, Johnson joined the science club and took a test to see how he would do as an engineer. Unfortunately, the results were not very good. "They told me I had little aptitude for engineering," he remembered. But Johnson's mother encouraged him to ignore the test results and continue to read and study. "It's what you put in your head that counts," she said. "Nobody can take that away from you."

As a high school senior, Johnson decided to enter the University of Alabama science fair. He was the only African-American contestant. Johnson searched in junkyards for parts to build a robot. Using compressed air, tape reels, and batteries, among other things, he constructed a remote-controlled robot that he named Linex. The robot moved on wheels powered by two motors, and a small tank of compressed air made the arms move. The robot spoke using a tape recorder and responded to voice commands through a walkie-talkie. As Johnson recalled, "Back then robots were unheard of, so I was one of only a few kids in the country who had their own robot." The robot won first prize in the science fair, which proved that Johnson had an aptitude for engineering. Still, he admitted that the experience was not as positive as it might have been: "[It] bothers me a little bit. If I had been [white] and did something as phenomenal as that, all sorts of doors would have opened."

In high school, Johnson joined the science club and took a test to see how he would do as an engineer. Unfortunately, the results were not very good. "They told me I had little aptitude for engineering," he remembered. But Johnson's mother encouraged him to ignore the test results and continue to read and study. "It's what you put in your head that counts," she said. "Nobody can take that away from you."

Johnson attended Tuskegee University in Alabama on a mathematics scholarship. While there, he was elected to the Pi Tau Sigma National Engineering Honor Society. He graduated with honors in 1972 with a bachelor's degree in mechanical engineering. Two years later he received a master of science degree in nuclear engineering.

CAREER HIGHLIGHTS

Soon after graduating from college, Johnson joined the U.S. Air Force. As a military engineer, he was quickly promoted to Advanced Space Systems Requirements officer at the Strategic Air Command in Omaha, Nebraska. In the 1980s, Johnson worked for the National Aeronautics and Space Administration (NASA) at the Jet Propulsion Laboratory (JPL) in Pasadena, California. At JPL, he worked on thermodynamic and control systems for space projects, including award-winning design work on the Galileo spacecraft that was sent to Jupiter. One of Galileo's design problems was that if the power supply were to fail in space, all the information stored in Galileo's computer would be lost. Johnson's co-workers were sure there was no way to build a power supply that would save Galileo's memory when power was lost. But Johnson and another engineer surprised everyone by building exactly such a power supply. Galileo was still orbiting Jupiter and storing data many years later, in the year 2000. "I tell this story because it sends a clear message to people to persevere," Johnson explained. During his time at JPL, he also worked on the Mars Observer project and the top-secret Stealth bomber.

> *In high school, Johnson constructed a remote-controlled robot that he named Linex. The robot moved, spoke, and responded to voice commands. As Johnson recalled, "Back then robots were unheard of, so I was one of only a few kids in the country who had their own robot."*

In his spare time, Johnson worked at his home, trying to invent a heat pump that would use water instead of freon to provide heating and cooling. Scientists had discovered that freon, which was used in nearly all refrigerators and air conditioners, was a threat to the environment. Freon is made of chloroflorocarbons (CFCs). When CFCs are released into the atmosphere, they cause damage to the ozone layer that helps protect the earth from the sun's radiation. Johnson was trying to find a replacement for freon that would be less toxic to the environment.

Inventing the Super Soaker

Johnson came up with his best-known invention completely by accident. One day in 1982, while working on the heat pump, he hooked a model of the pump to his bathroom sink. A stream of water shot across the bath-

room and into the tub with such force that the stream created a breeze that ruffled the curtains. "I thought, 'this would make a great water gun,'" Johnson recalled. He made a test model and gave it to his six-year-old daughter, Aneka, who went out to try it on the kids in the neighborhood. It was a great success. "The other kids couldn't even get close," Johnson laughed. "They just had regular water pistols."

Johnson's invention uses a plastic container to hold the water, an air pump, and a spring connected to the trigger. Below the barrel of the water gun is a sliding handle for the pump. When the handle is pushed back and forth, it fills the gun with air that is under pressure, like the air in a tire or a balloon. This pressure can be as much as 35 pounds per square inch. Pulling the trigger releases the water, and the air pressure causes it to rush out in a strong stream that can travel as far as 50 feet.

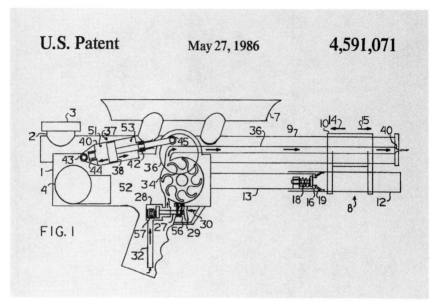

A diagram for the 1986 patent for Johnson's water gun.

Johnson called his invention the Pneumatic Water Gun and received a patent for it in 1986. A patent is a legal document that gives an inventor the sole right to make, use, and sell an invention for a limited period of time. The government registers the idea as the property of the inventor, and no other person or company is allowed to use it without the inventor's permission until the patent expires. After receiving his patent, Johnson looked into manufacturing the water gun himself. But he discovered that it would cost $200,000 to make the first 1,000 guns. To cover the manufacturing costs, he would have to charge $200 for each gun. He knew that no one would want to spend that much for a water gun. He needed to find a manufacturer that could produce his invention less expensively.

Bringing the Product to Market

Johnson's invention was completely new to the toy industry, and it took him years to bring it to market. At that point most water guns were small plastic pistol-type guns that didn't hold much water and couldn't shoot very far. There weren't particularly big sellers, and no one in the toy industry saw the potential until Johnson came along. Still, he wrote to nearly two dozen companies before he found one that agreed to make a version of his gun, calling it the Power Drencher. But the company soon went out of business. In 1989 Johnson took his design to the Toy Fair, an annual meeting attended by people from all aspects of the toy industry. There he met Al Davis, an owner of the Lamari Corporation in Philadelphia. Davis looked at the drawings and suggested that Johnson come and demonstrate his invention at the manufacturer's offices in Philadelphia.

Johnson showed up with a gadget built out of plastic plumbing pipe, a plastic Coke bottle, and Plexiglass. He and the Lamari officers went into a conference room. Johnson filled his gun with water, pumped it a few times, and the water shot across the large room. "We all said 'Wow!'" Davis recalled. The company agreed to manufacture the product and named it the Super Soaker. "I could sit here and say I was brilliant," Davis later said about Lamari's decision to market the toy, "but it was a simple thing, really. I liked it and I thought kids would like it." Lamari had already been manufacturing a long-range water gun, but it required batteries. The big advantages of the Super Soaker were that it did not require batteries, it held lots of water, and it did not need to be pumped very often — it held its pressure for a long time. They made sure to manufacture the squirt guns in bright colors and playful designs to avoid any confusion between these and real weapons.

The first Super Soakers appeared in stores in fall 1990. It was near the holiday season, but there was no guarantee the toy would sell because most kids are not interested in water pistols until the spring. In December, though, talk show host Johnny Carson brought out a Super Soaker on his late-night television show and used it to soak the audience. In England, newspapers showed pictures of Prince William and Prince Harry, the sons of Prince Charles and Princess Diana, carrying Super Soakers. Sales soared as a result of this publicity, and by 1992 the Super Soaker had earned more than $200 million in retail sales.

Meanwhile, Johnson quit his job as an aerospace engineer at the Jet Propulsion Laboratory and formed his own company, Johnson Research and Development. The purpose of the company was to conduct research leading to the invention of new products and technologies. Johnson wanted the inventions to be not only original and new, but to really stand out.

> When Johnson make his first test model of what would become the Super Soaker, he gave it to his six-year-old daughter, Aneka, who went out to try it on the kids in the neighborhood. It was a great success. "The other kids couldn't even get close," Johnson laughed. "They just had regular water pistols."

Soaker Problems

It was not long before other companies began to make water pistols that imitated the Super Soaker. Some of these products violated Johnson's patent. For example, one company sold a water gun called the Strong Shooter, which had a different shape and color scheme but used Johnson's idea. Other products were called names like Superpower 51 and Pump and Shoot Remco. Johnson hired lawyers to go to court to display diagrams of the real Super Soaker and show how the imitations illegally used his protected designs.

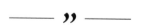

"It really revolutionized the water-gun marketplace," said Jim Silver, a toy-industry analyst who publishes the trade publication **Toy Book**. *"This is something that has been on our best-seller list every spring and summer since it was introduced."*

Unfortunately, Johnson's invention was not always used in the way it was intended, and this misuse sometimes led to tragedy. In Boston, a teenager was killed by another youth who, angry at being soaked, pulled out a real gun. In New York, a man hit with water from a Super Soaker shot two teenagers who were playing with the toy. In other cities, gangs filled the guns with chemicals like bleach or ammonia, which could hurt people if they were hit in the eyes. In Flint, Michigan, there were "drive-by" soakings—people driving by in cars and squirting people with the Soaker. In response, a Michigan lawmaker introduced legislation to outlaw the product's sale and use. But some felt that the attempts to ban the Soaker were misguided. One executive from Lamari phrased it like this: "We feel it's not the manufacture of toy guns that's the problem, but the misuse of them." As Johnson argued, "Why pick on a toy when it's not the toys that are doing the killing?"

Strong Sales

Many buyers seemed to agree, as sales continued to build each year. By 1995 sales of the Super Soaker were so strong that they had impressed the executives of Hasbro, a major toy manufacturer. Hasbro reached an agreement to purchase Lamari, making Lamari a subsidiary of Hasbro. Hasbro continued to employ Al Davis and the other Lamari officers who had demonstrated the good business sense to take Johnson's design and manufacture what has become his best-known invention.

The CPS 1700 carries an impressive 127 ounces of water and weighs over 11 pounds when full. With two nozzles to choose from, it delivers some serious soaking power.

Johnson has continued to make improvements to the Super Soaker over the years. He increased the range as well the amount of water the toy can hold. By 2000 there were many models of the Super Soaker available, ranging from basic Soakers costing a few dollars to the Super Charger Monster XL, which has 11 nozzles, holds more than a gallon of water, and costs $50. In addition, Johnson received a patent for another type of toy gun, also powered by compressed air, which shoots large foam pieces instead of water. It is estimated that more than 250 million Super Soakers have been sold since he invented the popular toy. "It really revolutionized the water-gun marketplace," said Jim Silver, a toy-industry analyst who publishes the trade publication *Toy Book*. "This is something that has been on our best-seller list every spring and summer since it was introduced." The Super Soaker is now the top-selling summer toy in the world.

Other Inventions

In addition to the Super Soaker, Johnson and his company, Johnson Research and Development, continued to work on other inventions. He worked on a new type of rechargeable battery, a digital thermostat, a home detector for radon (a radioactive gas that can harm people who are exposed to it), a wet diaper detector, hair-drying rollers, and a ground moisture sensor. Johnson also kept trying to make a water-based heat pump, the project he had been working on when he accidentally invented the Super Soaker.

Johnson visits a middle school with the Monster Super Soaker.

In 1993, Johnson's company announced the development of the Johnson Tube. The Johnson Tube is a heat pump that uses water instead of freon and is 25 percent more efficient than a freon pump. It can be used in heaters, refrigerators, and air conditioners. The pump heats water by forcing it through tiny holes so that it becomes water vapor. Then the water vapor goes through a pipe and collects at the bottom as hot water that can be used in the home. Because heat is transferred to the water, other parts of the system become cold and can be used for refrigeration. The company was awarded a contract with NASA to further develop the invention.

Currently, Johnson Research and Development continues to use technology in innovative and creative ways for both industrial and consumer projects. They develop environmental and energy related products in a range of areas, including thermodynamics, heat transfer, fluid dynamics, thermal hydraulics, digital circuit design, microprocessors, and control systems, among others. The company does ongoing research for NASA on the Johnson Tube. The company also continues to develop toys and other products for the consumer market. Today, Johnson holds over 40 patents, and he has over 20 more patents pending.

Johnson Research and Development is also preparing for a move. Currently located in Smryna, Georgia, the company has recently purchased a 170,000-square-foot property in Atlanta. The industrial and office property is located in an area of urban blight. Johnson plans to convert it into an upscale telecommunications and office center that will house Johnson Research and Development, as well as other high-tech firms. In the process, the company will work with a local training facility to train and hire many people from the neighboring community.

Winning Accolades and Acclaim

Johnson has won many honors for his success as an inventor, an entrepreneur, and a mentor to young people. He received one such honor when the mayor of Marietta, Georgia, where Johnson lived, declared February 25, 1994, to be Lonnie G. Johnson Day. He was honored not only for his business successes, but also for encouraging young people to invent. "Children are our future," he stated, "and I want to see them steered away from the negative influences I see them exposed to." His company, Johnson Research and Development, began conducting a program of workshops called Atlanta Community Entrepreneurs, or ACE. In these workshops, high-school students meet for 90 minutes to learn, talk about, and suggest the best ways to start their own business. They also listen to successful professionals who share their experiences and provide an example for the students. One of the best examples is surely that of Johnson himself, who took a simple mistake, turned it into an original idea, and persevered until he succeeded in creating one of the top-selling toys on the market.

"

Johnson encourages would-be inventors not to give up. "Stick to it," he urges. "It took me 10 years to make [the Super Soaker] work, and it wouldn't have happened without perseverance."

"

HOME AND FAMILY

The father of three children, Johnson now lives in Smyrna, Georgia, a suburb of Atlanta. His success has enabled him to spend as much time at home with his children as he likes. "Put it like this," he says of his company, "I could close this place down and go lay on the beach if I wanted to." He is not likely to do that, though, because he has lots of other ideas that he wants to work on. "A lot of people have ideas. The difference is following through on them," he explains. Johnson encourages would-be inventors not to give up. "Stick to it," he urges. "It took me 10 years to make [the Super Soaker] work, and it wouldn't have happened without perseverance."

AWARDS AND HONORS

Air Force Achievement Medal
Air Force Commendation Medal
NASA Achievement Award

FURTHER READING

Books

Amram, Fred M.B. *African-American Inventors,* 1996 (juvenile)

Periodicals

Black Enterprise, Nov. 1993, p.68
Chicago Tribune, July 28, 1991, p.C1; June 9, 1992, p.C1
Fort Worth Star Telegram, Feb. 1, 2000, p.10
Inventors' Digest, Mar./Apr. 1995, p.10
Los Angeles Times, May 9, 1991, p.J1; July 29, 1999, p.A1
Philadelphia Inquirer, Aug. 2, 1998, p.A1
San Francisco Chronicle, July 29, 1991, p.D3
Washington Post, June 13, 1992, p.B1

ADDRESS

Johnson Research and Development Company
1640 Roswell Street, Suite J
Smyrna, GA 30080

WORLD WIDE WEB SITES

http://www.johnsonrd.com/
http://web.mit.edu/invent/www/inventorsI-Q/johnson.html
http://www.invention-express.com/lonnieJohnson.html

Meg Lowman 1953-

American Botanist and Executive Director of Selby
Botanical Gardens in Florida
World-Famous Researcher of the Rainforest Canopy

BIRTH

Margaret Dalzell Lowman (pronounced LOO-man) was born
on December 23, 1953, in Elmira, New York. Her parents, John
and Alice Lowman, were both schoolteachers. She had two
younger brothers.

YOUTH

Lowman's lifelong love of nature began when she was young. A studious child, she filled her bedroom with small treasures she collected in the outdoors, including butterflies, birds' nests, shells, rocks, and flowers. She also enjoyed climbing trees and building forts and tunnels out of fallen branches. When Lowman was in the fourth grade, she and a small group of neighbor girls formed a Nature Club. They studied science, conducted experiments in their yards, and wrote little stories about their discoveries.

———— " ————

"I think science is really the way things work, and that's exciting," Lowman once said. "It is important to understand the bigger picture of our planet and where we live, how it functions, what we do with it, and how that will have impact."

———— " ————

EARLY INFLUENCES

As a young girl, Lowman admired two women who possessed great skills as natural scientists. One of these women was Rachel Carson, a biologist who wrote the 1962 book *Silent Spring* (for further information on Carson, see *Biography Today Environmental Leaders*, Vol. 1). *Silent Spring* alerted people to the dangerous effects of pesticides on animals and helped start the American environmental movement.

The other person Lowman admired was Harriet Tubman, an African-American woman who escaped from slavery in the 1850s and went on to became the most famous conductor on the Underground Railroad. This secret network of abolitionists (people who fought to end slavery) helped slaves escape from their masters and settle in the Northern United States and Canada, where slavery was not allowed. Tubman made 19 dangerous trips into slave territory and helped more than 300 slaves gain their freedom. A large part of her success was due to her outdoor knowledge and skills. For example, she was able to find her way through dark woods by feeling for moss growing on the north side of trees. She also knew which nuts, berries, and roots could be eaten along the way.

After learning about Carson and Tubman, Lowman became determined to build a career as a natural scientist. "I think science is really the way things work, and that's exciting," she stated. "It is important to understand the bigger picture of our planet and where we live, how it functions, what we do with it, and how that will have impact."

EDUCATION

Lowman was always an excellent student, especially in science. In the fifth grade, she won second place in the New York state science fair with a presentation about wildflowers. In high school at Elmira Free Academy, she became close friends with future fashion designer Tommy Hilfiger. After graduating as salutatorian of her class in 1972, Lowman earned a bachelor's degree in biology and environmental studies from Williams College in Massachusetts in 1976. Two years later, she earned a master's degree in ecology from the University of Aberdeen in Scotland.

After completing her master's, Lowman decided to work toward a Ph.D. At first, she hoped to make butterflies the subject of her doctoral studies. But since butterflies were difficult to find and catch, one of her professors convinced her to focus her research on trees instead. Lowman decided to study the rainforests of Australia while pursuing her doctorate degree at the University of Sydney. "From childhood on I loved trees. So there was a link from my youth, and I pursued forest ecology in college," she noted. "When I went overseas, it became apparent the rainforests were an up-and-coming issue of controversy and conservation." She eventually completed work on her Ph.D. in botany in 1983 in Sydney.

CAREER HIGHLIGHTS

Studying the Disappearing Rainforests

Rainforests are dense evergreen forests that typically grow in tropical regions that receive over 100 inches of rain each year. The warm, humid conditions in these regions support a tremendous variety of plant and animal life. In fact, rainforests cover just six percent of the earth's surface, but they contain more than 50 percent of the world's species of plants and animals. In addition to supporting diverse species, rainforests play an important role in regulating weather conditions around the globe. "The rainforest is like an air-conditioner for the planet," Lowman explained. "It influences our climate, our rainfall, our hurricane patterns."

Unfortunately, the world's rainforests are being destroyed at a rate per year of over 50,000 square miles—an area about the size of the state of Florida. The trees are being cut down by logging companies or burned down by local people in order to clear land for farming and grazing. Many of the world's most significant rainforests are located in countries where the people are poor and populations are rising rapidly. This situation creates a great deal of pressure to exploit the forests and other natural resources, because the local people need to use all the available resources just to support their families. According to some scientists, the rainforests could disappear completely within 25 years if this sort of activity continues.

Lowman is convinced that the loss of rainforests is already having negative effects on the planet. "By exploiting the forest, we're being bad air-conditioner technicians," she stated. "So suddenly we have global warming. We have rainfall patterns changing because we've removed the sponges that hold the clouds in place. I want people to understand just how integrated our planet is."

———— " ————

"The canopy represents one of the last frontiers of unknown science on the planet. Like the ocean bottom, the tops of trees are areas where very few people have ventured and very few people have made observations. There's an opportunity to describe new species and make new observations and discover new processes that could be extremely important for the way forest ecosystems function."

———— " ————

Lowman decided to concentrate her scientific research in the rainforests in order to prove how important they are and to encourage people to conserve them. Once she began studying the Australian rainforests, she became most interested in the upper layer of the trees, known as the rainforest canopy. No one had really studied the canopy—which ranges from 50 to 150 feet above the ground—until the late 1970s. But Lowman enjoyed being a pioneer in her field. "The canopy represents one of the last frontiers of unknown science on the planet," she explained. "Like the ocean bottom, the tops of trees are areas where very few people have ventured and very few people have made observations. There's an opportunity to describe new species and make new observations and discover new processes that could be extremely important for the way forest ecosystems function."

Struggling to Balance Work and Family

In the early 1980s, shortly after earning her doctorate degree from the University of Sydney, Lowman got a chance to use her knowledge to help solve a mystery. For several years, Australian eucalyptus trees had been dying in frightening numbers from an unknown disease. This problem was beginning to threaten the farming communities around Sydney. Some people in Australia worried that koala bears might be responsible for the

epidemic. But Lowman and her research partner, Harold Heatwold, discovered that a common beetle was causing the eucalyptus trees to die. The introduction of new farming and grazing practices had led to a rapid increase in beetle numbers, and the trees were unable to defend themselves.

In 1983, Lowman married an Australian sheep rancher who owned some of the forest land where she had been conducting her research. After giving birth to two sons, Edward and James, she discovered that her husband and his family held very traditional views about the role of women. They expected her to give up her career as a scientist in order to concentrate on being a wife and mother. At first, Lowman tried hard to make her marriage work. "I kept a *Journal of Ecology* wedged between the pages of my *Women's Weekly,* so that I could glance at scientific articles but appear to be studying the latest hints in home decorating," she admitted. She cooked, cleaned, sheared sheep, and performed all the duties of a farm wife. With no child care available, she carted the children along while she studied trees. Lowman felt that she could balance her work and family commitments, but her husband refused to consider this possibility. Over time, she grew more and more unhappy. "I came to the uncomfortable realization that my principles had been compromised," she recalled. "It was more important that I serve my husband morning tea and a hot lunch than it was to work on a scientific manuscript."

In 1990, Lowman was invited to join the faculty of Williams College in Massachusetts for six months as a visiting professor. Feeling exhausted, she welcomed the opportunity to return to the United States with her sons. The strong emotions she felt upon arriving convinced her that she had made the right decision. "When I reached the customs desk, the young officer looked me straight in the eye and said 'Welcome home.' I burst into tears," she remembered. Lowman never returned to Australia. Instead, she filed for divorce and committed herself to balancing her career as a scientist with her responsibilities as a single mother.

> Lowman's students found that flying squirrels — which were believed to be rare in Massachusetts — were actually abundant in the forest canopy. People only thought they were rare because no one had ever looked for them in the upper layers of the forest. "We forgot to look up," Lowman stated. "It's such a basic and obvious oversight."

Lowman taught at Williams College for two years. During this time, she was determined to help her students understand the importance of the forest canopy. She obtained a grant to build two 70-foot-high platforms connected by a 40-foot-long walkway in the middle of a forest of 100-year-old red oaks near campus. The students loved conducting scientific research in the treetops. They also made several interesting discoveries. For example, the students found that flying squirrels — which were believed to be rare in Massachusetts — were actually abundant in the forest canopy. People only thought they were rare because no one had ever looked for them in the upper layers of the forest. "We forgot to look up," Lowman stated. "It's such a basic and obvious oversight."

Traveling to Rainforests around the World

In 1992, Lowman left Williams College to become the director of research and conservation at Marie Selby Botanical Gardens in Sarasota, Florida. The facility, which opened in 1975, has 13 acres of rare and exotic plants from around the world. It also holds one of the world's largest catalogs of rainforest plant and insect samples. Lowman's job at Selby involved traveling to rainforest regions, conducting research on the canopy layer, and collecting more specimens from the treetops. She wanted to find and identify as many rare species of plants and animals as possible before the rainforests disappeared. She also hoped to discover species that had some sort of value—plants that could be used to make medicine, for example, or animals that would attract tourists—so the local people could make money by preserving the rainforest rather than exploiting it.

During the 1990s, Lowman's work took her to Belize and Panama in Central America, Peru in South America, and Cameroon in Africa. One of the most difficult obstacles to her research was finding a way to reach the treetops. She tried a number of different ground-based methods of studying the canopy, but she ultimately found that her only option was to climb up there. "I did not intend to climb trees as a career," she explained. "In fact, I tried desperately to think of alternatives to climbing—such as training a monkey, utilizing large telephoto cameras on pulleys, or working along cliff edges. None of these methods seemed feasible for accurate data collection, so I finally decided to become an arbornaut," Lowman said, using the unofficial name for scientists who explore the treetops, as astronauts explore the stars.

For one project, Lowman rode in the bucket of a construction crane to reach the forest canopy. For another, she conducted her research from a large plastic sled that was suspended from a hot-air balloon. She once rode into the treetops on an inflatable device that looked like a giant spider. More recently, she designed systems of treehouses and catwalks to connect various parts of the canopy. Even with these systems in place, however, she always wears a helmet and climbing harness to protect herself in case of a fall.

Much of Lowman's research has centered on epiphytes, unusual plants that attach themselves to the upper portions of trees in the rainforest. Epiphytes do not grow in soil like other plants. Instead, they extract nutrients and moisture from the air. Lowman has also studied the life cycle of leaves on trees. She discovered that leaves on the uppermost layer of trees only last two to three years, while leaves lower in the canopy can last more than ten years. Finally, Lowman has conducted research into the relationship between plants and insects in the canopy. She found a species of ant that lives in the upper reaches of trees and protects the trees against other insects and disease.

Lowman enjoys the unique perspective she gains in the treetops. "It's estimated that 95 percent of the organisms on the earth view life from 75 feet downwards, while humans are one of the few that view life from

about five feet high upwards," she noted. But her work is not always fun. In addition to the risk of falling, she also faces insect bites, rashes from contact with poisonous plants, problems from exposure to extreme heat and humidity, and encounters with dangerous snakes and scorpions.

In many cases, Lowman has been the only woman in a team of researchers. This sometimes made it difficult to find privacy for changing her clothes or taking a shower. But she believes that being a woman has also helped her connect with the local people in rainforest regions. "I think a woman sees things differently, and as a woman I've been overjoyed at the opportunity to work in some of these remote places around the world," she stated. "There are feelings of trust that women in these remote villages have for other women, and that makes a difference."

The JASON Project

Through her work in the rainforest canopy, Lowman has twice been involved with the JASON Project. This annual program was created by Robert Ballard, the scientific explorer who discovered the shipwreck of the *Titanic* (for further information on Ballard, see the entry in this volume of *Biography Today Scientists & Inventors*). The program was designed to increase young people's interest in science by providing them with the opportunity to work directly with scientists on projects at sites around the world. Student participants in the JASON

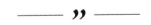

"I did not intend to climb trees as a career. In fact, I tried desperately to think of alternatives to climbing — such as training a monkey, utilizing large telephoto cameras on pulleys, or working along cliff edges. None of these methods seemed feasible for accurate data collection, so I finally decided to become an arbornaut,"Lowman said, using the unofficial name for scientists who explore the treetops, as astronauts explore the stars.

Project can watch special live broadcasts of scientific expeditions. They can also ask scientists questions via satellite and operate remote-control underwater probes. In addition, the JASON Project is now broadcast live over the Internet every year. More than five million children from the United States, the United Kingdom, and Mexico participated in the program during its first decade, and it's expected to reach millions more in the coming years. Certainly, the project has proven very popular with students.

Lowman has been involved with this program twice. She participated in JASON V, which investigated the health of our planet and the effect that people have on it. In 1994 she traveled to the Central American country of Belize to study the canopy of the diverse and pristine tropical rainforest. There, she studied the interaction between plants and insects in the canopy layer, trying to determine the size of the insect population and how it affects defoliation of the trees. This was part of her ongoing interest in comparing rates of insect defoliation in different rainforests in the Old World (Australia and Africa) and the New World (Panama, Costa Rica, Ecuador, Peru, and Belize). Lowman also participated in JASON X, a comparative study of three different types of rainforests. First, the researchers of JASON X traveled back in time to excavate an ancient rainforest site in Colorado from 63 millions years ago. Next, they explored the temperate rainforests of the Pacific Northwest. Finally, they investigated the tropical rainforests of Peru, where Lowman traveled in 1999. For this project, she had three specific areas of interest: the ecology of plants and insects in the rainforest canopy; the ecology of epiphytes, or air plants, surveying which epiphytes live in which forests; and the dynamics of species diversity, how so many species live together in the tropics.

> "I think a woman sees things differently, and as a woman I've been overjoyed at the opportunity to work in some of these remote places around the world. There are feelings of trust that women in these remote villages have for other women, and that makes a difference."

Promoting Rainforest Conservation

When she's not visiting rainforests around the world, Lowman has encouraged their conservation through her work at Selby Botanical Gardens. She organized two conferences, in 1994 and 1998, that attracted the 200 leading canopy researchers from around the world. These scientists shared their discoveries and discussed ways to preserve the rainforests. In 1999, Lowman was named executive director at Selby. She immediately launched a $15 million program to turn the facility into an international training center focusing on rainforest conservation. She hopes that someday scientists from Africa and South America will come to Selby to learn how to manage their forest resources for the future.

In her new position, Lowman is not able to travel as frequently as she once did. Instead, she spends a great deal of time attending fund-raisers

and forming connections between Selby and the Sarasota community. "I was perfectly happy in my old job. But so many people in the community encouraged me to go for this. I realized that I was already seen as a spokesman for Selby far more than I realized," she stated. "Rather than just sitting in my chair, and saying that I wished the community knew more about conservation, I decided I should jump in and get my feet muddy." The scientist, who wears only khaki clothing in the field, has made a splash at several recent social events in custom-made dresses designed by her friend Tommy Hilfiger.

Lowman has also brought public attention to rainforest conservation through a book and several television appearances. In 1999 she published her autobiography, *Life in the Treetops: Adventures of a Woman in Field Biology*. In this book, she discusses her research in the canopy, the importance of rainforest protection, the difficulties of being one of the only women in her field, and her struggles balancing career and family. *Life in the Treetops* received a glowing review in the *New York Times*, which praised her "wonderfully plain-spoken approach" and called the book a "funny, unassuming, and deeply idiosyncratic chronicle of her trials and triumphs as a field biologist." Lowman was surprised and gratified by all the attention her book received. "If I can explain science, I'm happy about that," she said modestly. "If I can make scientists seem human, I'm happy about that."

Also in 1999, Lowman was featured in "Heroes of the High Frontier," a televised *National Geographic* special. The show focused on her discovery of a previously unknown beetle species in the Amazon rainforest. "It has a great message," she said of the show. "They've done an excellent job of getting across to the public feelings of conservation and a passion and love for the rainforest."

———— " ————

"The problems of sampling in tall trees, in complex forests, in remote jungles, and often in the absence of any creature comforts created considerable adventure in my life. The personal issues of marriage, parenting, and women's roles as perceived by different cultures created additional barriers. But these issues also forced me to develop strong convictions as I made my choices along the pathway through adulthood."

———— " ————

To encourage Americans to support forest conservation, Lowman helped build a canopy walkway in Florida's Myakka River State Park in 2000. The 120-foot-long walkway—which resembles those she used during her research in South America—is situated high in a grove of cypress, pine, and oak trees. It is intended to allow anyone who can climb stairs to experience and appreciate the unique ecosystem of the forest canopy. "Our forests are as endangered as the rest," Lowman explained. "We want to enthuse people, to make them aware of the conservation of the forest in our own backyard." The staff of Selby Botanical Gardens is developing a curriculum that will enable students to use the walkway as an outdoor classroom.

Lowman admits that she faced a number of obstacles in building a career as a world-famous researcher of the rainforest canopy. But she says that overcoming these obstacles helped her become a stronger person. "The problems of sampling in tall trees, in complex forests, in remote jungles, and often in the absence of any creature comforts created considerable adventure in my life," she noted. "The personal issues of marriage, parenting, and women's roles as perceived by different cultures created additional barriers. But these issues also forced me to develop strong convictions as I made my choices along the pathway through adulthood."

MARRIAGE AND FAMILY

In 1983, Lowman married an Australian sheep rancher. They had two sons—Edward, born in 1985, and James, born in 1987—before divorcing in 1990. In October 1998, Lowman married attorney Michael Brown. Her second husband is very supportive of her career as a scientist. "On our first date, I took him up in the tree canopy at Selby Gardens," she recalled. "Everybody at Selby laughs at that. They say I was testing him."

Lowman lives in Sarasota, Florida, with her husband and sons. Their house is full of artifacts from her travels around the world, including a pet tarantula. In the backyard, the family has built a rope bridge between two large oak trees so that everyone can spend time in the forest canopy. Her sons usually accompany her on one research trip per year. When Lowman travels without them, the boys are cared for by her husband, brother, or parents.

HOBBIES AND OTHER INTERESTS

When Lowman is not traveling to study rainforests around the world, she enjoys being at home with her family. She lifts weights and jogs every morning to stay in shape for the vigorous work of climbing trees.

SELECTED WRITINGS

Forest Canopies, 1995
Life in the Treetops: Adventures of a Woman in Field Biology, 1999

HONORS AND AWARDS

Explorers Club: 1997
Visionary Award (Girls Inc.): 2000
Books for the Teen Age (New York Public Library): 2000, for *Life in the Treetops*

FURTHER READING

Books

Lasky, Kathryn. *The Most Beautiful Roof in the World: Exploring the Rainforest Canopy,* 1997 (juvenile)
Lowman, Margaret D. *Life in the Treetops: Adventures of a Woman in Field Biology,* 1999

Periodicals

Discover, Nov. 1, 1995, p.92
Garbage, Oct.-Nov. 1992, p.13
New York Times, Feb. 22, 1994, p.C1; Nov. 22, 1994, p.C1
St. Petersburg Times, June 14, 1992, p.F1; Feb. 27, 1994, p.F5; Aug. 18, 1999,
    p.D1
Sarasota Herald-Tribune, Jan. 21, 1996, p.A1; Jan. 27, 1999, p.B1; Mar. 28,
    1999, p.B11; June 27, 1999, p.E1; Aug. 13, 1999, Ticket Section, p.24;
    Feb. 22, 2000, p.B1; Mar. 26, 2000, p.E1
Science News, Dec. 18, 1993, p.408
Scientific American, Dec. 1999, p.40
Tampa Tribune, Sep. 21, 1999, Baylife Section, p.1; Nov. 5, 1994, Home
    Section, p.8

ADDRESS

Marie Selby Botanical Gardens
811 S. Palm Ave.
Sarasota, FL 34236

e-mail: mlowman@selby.org

WORLD WIDE WEB SITES

http://www.jasonproject.org
http://www.selby.org

Forrest Mars Sr. 1904-1999

American Businessman and President of Mars
Candy Company
Inventor of M&Ms Candy

BIRTH

Forrest Edward Mars Sr. was born in 1904 in the area of
Minneapolis, Minnesota. He was the only child of Frank C.
Mars, a candy maker, and Ethel G. (Kissack) Mars. His exact
date of birth is a mystery, as are many other details of his
childhood and later life.

YOUTH

Forrest Mars endured a difficult childhood. His father owned a small candy-making company, but he struggled to make the enterprise a success. In fact, he poured nearly all of his money into the candy business, leaving little money for the basic food, shelter, and clothing needs of his family. This situation angered and frustrated Forrest's mother, and his parents' marriage eventually collapsed under the weight of the family's financial problems. In 1910 his mother divorced his father on grounds of nonsupport and gained sole custody of Forrest.

Ethel Mars loved her son, but she decided that she would not be able to provide him with a stable and comfortable home environment for a while. With this in mind, she reluctantly sent Forrest to live with his maternal grandparents in North Brattleford, Saskatchewan, a mining town in Canada. Once he settled in to North Brattleford, Forrest rarely saw or heard from his father. His mother, on the other hand, wrote him long letters and sent him money whenever she could spare it. But she could not afford to make many visits to Saskatchewan, so he rarely saw her either.

As Forrest grew older, he developed into a bright and competitive young man. He loved to play chess and cribbage, and often beat adults that he played. He also enjoyed dazzling people with trivia that he had memorized or information that he had learned from reading adult-level books. In fact, he became quite proud of his intelligence and knowledge, displaying his smarts at every opportunity. Around this same time, Forrest developed a strong sense of ambition and drive. This aspect of his personality may have been due in part to his mother's influence. She repeatedly referred to his father as a "miserable failure," and she always urged her son to work hard and make something of himself.

EDUCATION

Mars received his elementary education in a remote, one-room schoolhouse just outside of North Battleford, Saskatchewan. Each day, he walked or skied three miles to and from the little school, even on very cold and snowy winter days. His best subject was mathematics, but he earned excellent grades in most other subjects as well. After completing elementary school, he attended Lethbridge High School in Alberta. He once again emerged as a star student, and during his senior year he won a partial scholarship to attend the University of California. Mars graduated from Lethbridge in 1922.

One year later, Mars enrolled at the University of California at Berkeley to study mining. Soon after beginning his classes, he took a part-time job in the school cafeteria so that he could pay for his room and board. At first, his work responsibilities amounted to little more than scrubbing floors and washing dishes. Within months of his arrival, though, he managed to gain a campus-wide reputation as a smart young businessman. He showed the school chef how to change menus so that he could use more meats that were available at big discounts. Mars arranged the meat purchases, then pocketed a big percentage of the profits. Before long he was making $100 a week at a time when many adults did not make that much money in a month of full-time work.

After completing his freshman year, Forrest visited Chicago, where he was reunited with his father. It had been years since he had seen Frank Mars, and his father's life had changed dramatically during that time. He had remarried and established a very successful candy-making business in the Minneapolis area. "[This] was not a story that Forrest was prepared for," wrote Joël Glenn Brenner in *The Emperors of Chocolate*. "Frank said nothing of his disappearance from Forrest's life. And perhaps afraid of the answers, Forrest, too, asked little about the past. Instead, the two men talked about business, the only neutral topic they had in common."

At Yale, Mars impressed his instructors with his dedication and passion for business. "I wanted to learn about money, about business," he later recalled. "I wasn't at Yale to be pampered, like some other boys."

Forrest later claimed that it was during this conversation that he gave his father the idea for the Milky Way bar. This candy bar, which featured a combination of chocolate coating and malted "nougat"—a mix of whipped egg whites and corn syrup—was introduced to the public by his father a year later, in 1924. The big bar, which actually cost less to produce than other bars because of its inexpensive ingredients, was a tremendous success. The Milky Way immediately became Frank Mars's most popular candy item, with sales of $800,000 in its first year of release. In fact, it proved so popular that Forrest's father was able to build a new candy-making plant in Chicago and move his business there.

Forrest, meanwhile, returned to California to continue his schooling. In 1925, however, Mars decided to transfer to Yale University, where he hoped to learn more about economics and business. He promptly enrolled in the industrial engineering program at Yale's Sheffield Scientific School. As he continued his studies, he impressed his instructors with his dedication and passion for business. "I wanted to learn about money, about business," Mars later recalled. "I wasn't at Yale to be pampered, like some other boys." He excelled in his classes and graduated from Yale in 1928.

CAREER HIGHLIGHTS

Joining His Father's Candy Company

After graduating, Mars went to work for his father in Chicago. By this time, the popularity of the Milky Way had transformed his father's company, known as Mars Inc., into one of the largest candy makers in America. The company became even more dominant during the early 1930s, when it introduced both the Snickers Bar (in 1930) and the Three Musketeers Bar (in 1932).

During this same time, though, the personal relationship between Forrest Mars and his father turned sour. Forrest disapproved of many of the company's rules and candy production guidelines. He felt that the factory operated inefficiently, and that new regulations and instructions should be introduced so that Mars Inc. could be even more profitable. But his interference plunged the factory into confusion and turmoil. Forrest's superior attitude and critical remarks sparked resentment among factory workers, and his attempts to change major aspects of the candy-making operation to his own taste infuriated his father. Forrest finally wore out his welcome in 1932, when he demanded that his father give him one-third of the company and allow him to expand the business into Canada. "This company isn't big enough for both of us," responded his father. "Go to some other country and start your own business."

In 1932 Forrest Mars resettled in England, where he hoped to make his own mark as a candy-maker and businessman. But his father did not send him away empty-handed. He gave Forrest $50,000, the Milky Way recipe, and foreign rights to produce the Milky Way bar. Armed with these materials, he was able to set up a candy manufacturing plant in an old warehouse outside London. He then sweetened up the chocolate in his Milky Way bars in order to satisfy the tastes of English candy consumers. Before long, Forrest's Milky Ways ranked among England's most popular candy bars. "If you make a really good product that people want and are willing to pay for, money will come," he commented in a 1966 interview in *Candy Industry and Confectioner's Journal,* the only interview he ever granted.

In 1934 Frank Mars died of kidney failure in Chicago. When he died, he gave his only son partial ownership of Mars Inc. But he left the majority of

his stock to his second wife—also named Ethel—and their daughter, Patricia (Forrest's half-sister). This settlement dissatisfied Forrest, and he spent the next two decades battling to gain possession of his father's company from the family of his father's second wife.

In the meantime, Mars continued to build a business empire in Europe. In 1934 he used his profits from the candymaking business to purchase Chappel Brothers, a small British dog food company. Within a few years, he built the company into a dominant force under the name Petfoods, Limited.

Introducing M&Ms

In the late 1930s Mars decided to begin production of a new candy that eventually came to be known as M&Ms. The origins of M&Ms are shrouded in mystery to this day. Some accounts suggest that the Mars candy was actually a version of a British candy called Smarties. But Forrest Mars strongly denied that he stole or bought the M&M idea from another company. He always claimed that he was inspired to make M&Ms after a late-1930s visit to Spain, where a civil war was raging. According to his account, he met several soldiers during his trip who were eating little pieces of chocolate coated with sugary candy. Mars noticed that the sugary coating not only added to the taste of the candy, but also kept the chocolate from melting quickly. He claimed that after returning to England, he immediately went to work on producing his own version of these tasty treats.

> At the M&Ms factory, "Explosive fits of screaming and cursing pierced the order of the factory floor several times a day. It seemed anything could set [Mars] off when he arrived at the factory. An employee who forgot to wash his hands, a messy pile of papers on a salesman's desk, or a speck of chocolate on a uniform could send him reeling into an abusive rage. Most workers eventually learned to shrug off these episodes, waiting patiently with heads bowed until the blood rushed out of Forrest's face and the taunts and name-calling ceased, almost as abruptly as they had begun." – Joël Glenn Brenner, **The Emperors of Chocolate**

In any case, when Mars returned to the United States in 1939 at the start of World War II, he was determined to begin production of M&Ms. Shortly after resettling in America — leaving his European operations in the hands of trusted managers — he invited a young businessman named R. Bruce Murrie to be a partner in the new candy-making venture. Mars chose Murrie because he was the son of the president of the Hershey candy company, the largest producer of chocolate in America. Murrie's involvement assured that Mars would have a steady supply of cocoa — the main ingredient in chocolate — during World War II, when many food manufacturers experienced shortages of basic ingredients.

Over the next two years, Mars and Murrie worked hard to build a facility that could make the candy-coated chocolates. The partners decided to call both their company and their product "M&Ms" in recognition of the initials of their last names. They built a plant in Newark, New Jersey, and built a big distribution network that would enable them to send the candies all across the country. During this time, Murrie's links to the Hershey company proved invaluable.

Hershey engineers helped design and install M&M production equipment and provided a great deal of technical assistance and advice to the two men.

M&Ms began appearing on store shelves in 1941, and they were an immediate hit. The candies were popular with both children and parents. Kids liked them because they were so tasty, and parents appreciated the fact that they were less messy than many other chocolate treats. These first M&Ms came in a variety of colors, but they did not feature the trademark M that now appears on the shell. In addition, the first M&Ms were a little larger than today's candies. But in most respects, the candy was the same as it is today.

The partnership between Mars and Murrie lasted only a few years, however. During the mid-1940s, the two men clashed so often that Murrie decided to sell all of his ownership stock in the company to Mars for $1 million. This purchase made Mars the sole owner of M&Ms.

A Talented but Temperamental Businessman

Mars guided his various companies to new levels of prosperity in the 1940s. During this time, he instituted policies at all of his plants in the United States and England to ensure high quality and workplace efficiency. He also made effective use of advertising to increase the popularity of M&Ms and other goods produced by his various companies. And he continued to branch out into other areas of food manufacturing. In 1942, for example, he took advantage of a new refining process for rice that made it more nutritious and easier to cook. Mars bought a rice mill and launched the Uncle Ben's Rice product line. Today, this brand remains one of the top-selling rice products in the world.

But Mars also became known as a fearsome boss with a terrible temper during this period. In fact, his temper tantrums became legendary among the employees who worked at his M&Ms factory. "Explosive fits of screaming and cursing pierced the order of the factory floor several times a day [at the M&Ms factory]," Brenner reported in her book *The Emperors of Chocolate*. "It seemed anything could set [Mars] off when he arrived at the factory. An employee who forgot to wash his hands, a messy pile of papers on a salesman's desk, or a speck of chocolate on a uniform could send him reeling into an abusive rage. Most workers eventually learned to shrug off these episodes, waiting patiently with heads bowed until the blood rushed out of Forrest's face and the taunts and name-calling ceased, almost as abruptly as they had begun." Some of Mars's employees attributed his actions to his high standards and insistence on quality. But others argued that he simply behaved like a mean and ruthless bully. "He treated everybody in the world like they were stupid—except him," claimed one former employee.

Building an Empire

During the late 1940s Mars combined his many business interests in the United States and Europe into a company called Food Manufacturers Inc. In 1949 he bought a 740-acre estate in Virginia for himself and his family. But Mars still spent much of the following decade inspecting his factory operations and devising new business strategies to increase the size of his empire. His most spectacular success during this period came in 1954, when he launched a peanut version of M&Ms in the U.S. market. Within two years, M&M sales topped $40 million. These sales made M&Ms the most popular candy in the United States, a position it continued to hold in the late 1990s.

In 1964, Mars finally succeeded in gaining ownership of his father's old Chicago company after more than two decades of legal battles with the family of Frank Mars's second wife. The relatives agreed to sell all their stock in the company to Forrest Mars, provided that he change the name of his corporation from Food Manufacturers Inc. to Mars Inc. Forrest quickly agreed, and within a matter of months he merged the companies together into one giant food manufacturing concern.

A few days after buying the Chicago factory, Mars arrived at the plant for a get-acquainted meeting with the company's management. At the start of the meeting, however, he reportedly shocked the gathered executives by falling to his knees and praying for all of the Mars candy products by name, one by one: "I pray for Milky Way. I pray for Snickers. . . ." This startling display made the assembled executives realize that their new boss was intensely dedicated to his business operations.

Making Changes at Mars

As soon as Forrest Mars bought his father's old company, he instituted dramatic changes in its operation from top to bottom. He tore out all the factory offices and eliminated the executive dining room so that all employees—from inexperienced clerks to high-level officers—worked and ate together. He also instituted a time card policy for everyone, including the company's top executives, to keep track of the hours that his employees worked. Finally, Mars introduced extremely high standards of cleanliness, efficiency, and quality to the entire factory operation. In return for working under these demanding conditions, Mars employees received good benefits, generous salaries, and opportunities for substantial financial bonuses when the company performed well.

Mars Inc. thrived during Forrest Mars's first years of leadership and became an industry trailblazer in a number of areas. For instance, Mars became the first candy company in the country to date its product for freshness. The company also became the first candy-maker to limit the amount of time that its products could sit on store shelves before being removed. In addition, Mars automated his factories earlier than any of his competitors. "He was way ahead of everyone when it came to equipment," recalled one former Mars manager in an interview with Brenner. "He had solved engineering problems that no one else had even considered tackling." Moreover, the company made tremendously effective use of television as an advertising tool throughout the 1960s. It was during this period, for instance, that the company introduced the famous M&Ms slogan "it melts in your mouth, not in your hands."

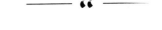

Some of Mars's employees attributed his actions to his high standards and insistence on quality, while others argued that he simply behaved like a mean and ruthless bully. "He treated everybody in the world like they were stupid — except him," claimed one former employee.

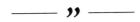

But Mars's intense personality and demanding standards continued to make him a difficult man to work for. This was especially true for his two sons — Forrest Jr. and John — who had started to work for the company. They received particularly rough treatment from their father. "He was terrible to them," recalled one longtime Mars executive. "He would shout and call them dumb and stupid. He would harangue them over the smallest detail. Everyone in the room would fall silent, and you could hear him screaming all the way into the factory. It was horribly embarrassing." One of his sons reportedly displeased his father so greatly during one 1964 meeting of company managers that Mars Sr. ordered him to kneel on the floor and pray for the future of the company. He then resumed the meeting, leaving the young man to kneel silently on the floor for an hour in front of his co-workers. The son reportedly rose to his feet only after his father called an end to the meeting and walked out of the conference room.

A Secretive Man and Company

By the time Forrest Mars acquired his father's old company in 1964, he also had acquired a reputation as an extremely secretive man. This aspect of his personality remained strong throughout his long career, from the 1940s until his death in 1999. He allowed himself and his family to be photographed on only a few occasions, and he gave only one interview in his entire life. This interview, given to an industry magazine called *Candy Industry and Confectioner's Journal,* took five years for the magazine's editors to arrange. When the interview was published in 1966, Mars angrily charged that he had been misquoted. He then vowed never to give another interview.

Mars's secretive nature, which seemed based on both a genuine desire for privacy and deep suspicion of others, led him to institute a number of strict rules on his employees over the years. For example, Mars employees were threatened with instant dismissal from their jobs if they talked about him or various aspects of corporate operations to people outside the company. He also barred non-employees from Mars factories around the world. And officials at Mars refused to provide any information on their mysterious owner, from his exact date of birth to whether he was even still alive.

Mars's attitude eventually filtered down to his sons, who have also avoided reporters and other outsiders over the years. But his sons are less rigid in this area than their father, and they have occasionally tried to explain their publicity-shy ways. "Privacy at times today seems a relic of the non-media past," explained Forrest Jr. in a rare speech. "But it is a legal right — morally and ethically proper and even desirable — and a key to healthy, normal living. [Privacy] allows us to do the very best we can, the very best we know how, and to do so without being concerned with self-aggrandizement."

Starting a New Business

In 1973 Mars Sr. turned over day-to-day management of the Mars empire to his sons. But their father continued to take an active role in corporate decision-making. His continued involvement apparently angered both Forrest Jr. and John. In fact, Mars employees reportedly did not dare to even mention Forrest Mars's name to his sons out of fear that it would push them into dark and angry moods.

Mars Inc. thrived under Forrest Mars and became an industry trailblazer in a number of areas: in dating products for freshness, in limiting the time that products sat on store shelves, and in automating his factories. "He was way ahead of everyone when it came to equipment," recalled one former Mars manager in an interview. "He had solved engineering problems that no one else had even considered tackling."

In 1980 Mars Sr. finally stopped involving himself in the affairs of the Mars candy empire and announced his full retirement. That same year, Mars Inc. refused to allow M&Ms to be used in the motion picture *E.T.* as the lovable alien's favorite treat. This decision drew harsh criticism when Reese's Pieces, which were substituted for M&Ms, enjoyed a surge of popularity after the movie's release.

But despite this misstep and reports of a bitter power struggle between Forrest Jr. and John for control of the company, the Mars empire remained strong. In fact, it retained its rank as the nation's top candy manufacturer throughout the 1980s and 1990s, with five of America's top ten selling products (Snickers, M&M Peanuts, M&M Plain, Three Musketeers, and Milky Way). In addition, it continued to produce many other popular food items, including Dove ice cream bars, the pretzel snack Combos, the Uncle Ben's line of rice dishes, and pet food products under the Whiskas, Sheba, and Pedigree brands. In fact, by the late 1980s, *Fortune* magazine estimated that earnings from these popular products had transformed the Mars family into the richest family in the United States.

> "He was one of a kind, one of those great entrepreneurs you read about in history books. He was one of the most astute businessmen I've ever met, just brilliant."
> — Somer Hollingsworth, president of the Nevada Development Authority

Meanwhile, Mars Sr. decided that he did not like being retired. In 1981 the restless billionaire established a new company called Ethel M Chocolates in Henderson, Nevada, to make fancy liqueur-flavored chocolates. The facility for this new venture, which Mars Sr. named for his mother, cost more than $6 million to build. It included not only the world's best candy-making machinery, but also a special apartment above the factory floor where he could live. Once the plant opened, he spent nearly all of his time in this apartment, which featured one-way glass so that he could watch the workers as they made the candies. This arrangement struck many employees as strange and vaguely creepy, and some of them started referring to Mars Sr. as "the phantom of the candy factory."

In 1990 Mars Sr. sold his Ethel M Chocolates business to Mars Inc. When he told his sons that he wanted to continue living in his factory penthouse, though, they insisted that he pay them rent. Mars Sr. did not like this condition, and he moved to Miami a short time later. In 1994 he suffered a stroke, and he spent his final years in a wheelchair as a reclusive tycoon — *Forbes* magazine estimated in 1996 that he had a net worth of $3 billion. He died of natural causes on July 1, 1999, in Miami.

After the death of Forrest Mars Sr., many people hailed him as one of America's most innovative and dedicated businessmen. "He was one of a kind, one of those great entrepreneurs you read about in history books," said Somer Hollingsworth, president of the Nevada Development Authority. "He was one of the most astute businessmen I've ever met, just brilliant." A few months later, in December 1999, his sons gave Yale University $2 million to establish a professorship in ethics, politics, and economics at the school in honor of their father. "John and I decided to establish a lasting tribute to our father's memory that will also reflect his dedication to Yale," announced Forrest Mars Jr. "After considering a range of possible programs, we settled on the undergraduate major in ethics, politics, and economics because of our father's and our own strong interest in these issues."

MARRIAGE AND FAMILY

Forrest Mars Sr. married Audrey Meyer in 1930. They had three children, Forrest Jr., John, and Jacqueline (Jackie). Audrey Meyer died of cancer on June 1, 1989.

HONORS AND AWARDS

U.S. Business Hall of Fame (*Fortune* magazine): 1984

FURTHER READING

Books

Brenner, Joël Glenn. *The Emperors of Chocolate,* 1999
Fucini, Joseph J. *Entrepreneurs: The Men and Women Behind Famous Brand Names and How They Made It,* 1985
Ingham, John N., and Lynne B. Feldman. *Contemporary American Business Leaders: A Biographical Dictionary,* 1990
Pottker, Jan. *Crisis in Candyland,* 1995
Who's Who in America, 1997

Periodicals

Atlantic, Oct. 1988, p.34
Business Week, Aug. 14, 1978, p.52
Candy Industry and Confectioner's Journal, 1966
Forbes, Oct. 14, 1996, p.116; Dec. 13, 1999, p.178
Fortune, May 31, 1982, p.114; Apr. 2, 1984, p.106; Sep. 26, 1988, p.98; Nov. 28, 1994, p.82
Los Angeles Times, July 3, 1999, p.C1
New York Times, Feb. 22, 1998, section 14, p.3; July 3, 1999, p.B7

U.S. News and World Report, Aug. 9, 1999, p.42
Wall Street Journal, July 6, 1999, p.A22
Washington Post, July 3, 1999, p.A1; July 6, 1999, p.E1
Washington Post Magazine, Apr. 12, 1992, p.11
Washingtonian, Jan. 1996, p.59

WORLD WIDE WEB SITE

http://www.mars.com

Akio Morita 1921-1999

Japanese Electronics Engineer and Businessman
Co-Founder of Sony Corporation

BIRTH

Akio Morita was born on January 26, 1921, in Kasugaya, Japan. His father, Kyuzaemon Morita, owned a company that produced the traditional Japanese rice wine called sake (pronounced sock-ee). His mother, Shuko (Toda) Morita, was a homemaker. Akio had two younger brothers, Kazuaki and Masaaki, and one sister, Kikuko.

YOUTH

Morita was born into a wealthy family that had brewed sake since the 1600s. As the oldest son, he was expected to take over the family business when he grew up. His father began teaching him to run the company from the time he was a boy. "My father expected me to succeed him in his business," Morita explained. "So even when I was a primary school student, he took me to his office and made me sit beside him. He conducted conferences, took me to the bank, and tried to educate me as the top management."

But young Morita found learning about the sake business rather dull. He was much more interested in electronics, especially after his family got an RCA Victrola record player. "My father bought the first electronic phonograph for us," he recalled. "And that gave us fantastic sound which, in fact, impressed me so much that I started to wonder how or why such a sound came out. That's where my interest in electronics began." From then on, Morita spent all of his spare time reading *Popular Mechanics* and technical books. He used this information to build his own record player and ham radio transmitter.

EDUCATION

Morita was an extremely bright young man, but his fascination with electronics got in the way of his schoolwork. "In high school, we had no chance to study electronic technology, so I bought many, many books about it," he noted. "My grades began to suffer, as I spent all my time studying electronics." Morita was forced to put aside his hobby for a year in order to qualify to attend the prestigious Eighth Higher School, which is similar to an American preparatory school. "I became the lowest-ranking graduate of my school ever to be admitted to the science department of the Eighth Higher School and it took me a year of extra study to make it," he admitted.

After graduating from the Eighth Higher School, Morita went on to earn a degree in physics at Osaka Imperial University in 1944. World War II was raging at the time, and Japan and Germany were fighting against the U.S., England, France, Soviet Union, and other Allied nations. So Morita joined the Imperial Japanese Navy and was stationed at the Naval Research Center in Susaki, Japan. Working as an engineer, he helped develop heat-seeking weapon systems and night-vision gunsights for the Japanese military. It was during his military service that Morita met Masaru Ibuka, a senior engineer who shared his interest in electronics and who would soon become his business partner.

CAREER HIGHLIGHTS

Starting a Small Electronics Company

In 1946, after the end of the war, Morita and Ibuka decided to form their own company to make electronic equipment. Before he could go into business with his friend, though, Morita had to convince his father to allow his younger brother Kazuaki to become the head of the family sake business. Morita's new company, Tokyo Tsushin Kogyo Kabushiki Kaisha (Tokyo Telecommunications Company), set up shop in a burned-out department store in Tokyo using $500 borrowed from Morita's family. They started out by producing amplifiers, communication devices, and voltmeters (instruments that measure differences in voltage or current at points in an electrical circuit).

Morita's company struggled through its first few years in business. Tokyo Telecommunications Company was able to sell a few electronic devices to Japanese government agencies, but the founders really wanted to break into the consumer electronics market. Their first product intended for use in people's homes was a tape recorder. Unfortunately, the tape recorder they produced was very heavy and expensive, and no one saw a need for it. But Morita learned a valuable lesson from the experience. "Having unique technology and being able to make unique products are not enough to keep a business going," he stated. "You have to sell the products, and to do that you have to show the potential buyer the real value of what you are selling."

"In high school, we had no chance to study electronic technology, so I bought many, many books about it. My grades began to suffer, as I spent all my time studying electronics."

In 1952, Morita and Ibuka read about a breakthrough in electronics, called a transistor, that had been developed

Morita presenting a new Sony seven-inch portable color TV set, 1967.

by Bell Laboratories of the United States. Transistors are tiny solid-state electronic devices that amplify or increase voltage and current. At first, most electronics experts did not think that transistors would find many uses in consumer products. But Morita and Ibuka believed that they could use transistors to create a new, portable radio. Tokyo Telecommunications Company signed an agreement that gave them the right to manufacture the technology in Japan. After several years of research and development, they produced the first AM transistor radio in 1955. They followed this innovation with a popular pocket-sized radio in 1957 and the first FM transistor radio in 1958.

Becoming the Marketing Man for Sony

In 1958, Morita and Ibuka decided to change the name of their company. They wanted a name that would be easy for people to say and remember, both in Japan and in other countries around the world as the company expanded. They finally settled on the name Sony, which they created by combining *sonus,* the Latin word for sound, with the English nickname *sonny.* At this point, the founding partners of Sony decided to concentrate on separate areas of the business. Ibuka continued working on the technical side, conducting research and developing new electronic products. In the meantime, Morita changed his focus to marketing the company's products and developing the overall business.

One of Morita's first missions involved finding a way to sell his company's products in the United States. "Our first transistor radio of 1955 was small and practical," he recalled. "I saw the U.S. as a natural market; business was booming, employment was high, the people were progressive and eager for new things." But Morita faced a significant obstacle in selling Sony products to American consumers. At that time, many people viewed Japanese goods as inferior in quality and reliability. "'Made in Japan' was regarded as meaning very cheap, poor quality," he admitted.

"Having unique technology and being able to make unique products are not enough to keep a business going. You have to sell the products, and to do that you have to show the potential buyer the real value of what you are selling."

One possible way around the problem was to license Sony products to a well-known and respected manufacturer. Morita spoke with representatives from Bulova, a large electronics company with 50 years of experience in the industry. They were impressed with Sony's transistor radio and offered to buy 100,000 units to sell in the U.S. market. The deal would have been a huge financial success for Sony, but Morita rejected it because the Bulova representatives insisted on putting the Bulova name on the products.

Morita felt it was important to build the Sony brand name for the future, even if it cost the company some sales in the present. "Fifty years ago," he told the people from Bulova, "your brand name must have been just as unknown as our name is today. I am here with a new product, and I am now taking the first step for the next 50 years of my company. Fifty years from now, I promise you that our name will be just as famous as your company name is today." It turned out to be a wise decision, as the transistor radio sold well and helped bring widespread attention to Sony.

To gain an understanding of American tastes, Morita moved to the United States with his family in the early 1960s. They lived in a fancy apartment in the Manhattan section of New York City for over a year. During this time, Morita set up an American branch of his company called Sony Corporation of America. In 1963, it became the first Japanese-based company to sell stock in the United States. Seven years later, Sony became the first Japanese company to be listed on the New York Stock Exchange, the largest and most prestigious financial market in the world.

> *"Our first transistor radio of 1955 was small and practical," he recalled. "I saw the U.S. as a natural market; business was booming, employment was high, the people were progressive and eager for new things."*

Making Sony a World Leader in Consumer Electronics

Throughout the 1960s, Sony continued to make technological advances and introduce popular new products to the American market. For example, the company expanded its use of transistor technology into videotape recorders and portable television sets. In 1969, Sony launched the Trinitron color television set. This television used a revolutionary new picture tube called the Chromatron, which projected a picture on the screen that had bolder and more realistic colors than were ever possible before. Within a short time, sales of the Trinitron topped the best-known American television brands, like RCA and Zenith.

By the 1970s, the success of Sony and other companies had completely changed the image of Japanese products. Now many U.S. consumers viewed Japanese goods as superior in quality and reliability to American-made products. In addition, Japanese products were often less expensive than similar American goods because the manufacturers had lower labor costs than U.S. firms. As a result, sales of Japanese products soared, while American companies suffered dramatic losses in market share. U.S. producers had controlled 98 percent of the worldwide consumer electronics market in the mid-1950s, for example, but lost 90 percent of their share over the next 20 years.

*Morita with a revolutionary new single unit video camera
and cassette recorder, 1980.*

As more U.S. factories closed and more Americans lost their jobs, many people began calling for increased taxes on goods imported from Japan. In addition, the U.S. Department of Justice accused several large Japanese companies (but not Sony) of "dumping," or selling products on the American market at a lower price than they were sold in Japan. This illegal practice was intended to increase the producers' share of the U.S. market and drive American competitors out of business.

This was a difficult time for Sony and other Japanese companies. But Morita—who became president of the company in 1971 and chief executive officer in 1976—refused to apologize for his country's dominance of U.S. markets. He claimed that Japanese companies simply produced "good quality products that people want and in such variety that any consumer whim can be satisfied. This is how Japanese goods managed to take so much of the U.S. market. . . . We did not 'invade' the American market as it is sometimes charged; we just sent our very best products to America." But Morita also took steps to ease the minds of Americans who worried about losing U.S. jobs to Japanese competition. In 1972, Sony built the first of several manufacturing plants in the United States.

Developing the Sony Walkman

Under Morita's guidance, Sony developed one of its most successful products in the 1970s. His philosophy was to develop cutting-edge products and then convince people to buy them, rather than relying on market research to determine consumers' needs. "Our plan is to lead the public with new products rather than ask them what kind of products they want," he explained. "The public does not know what is possible, but we do."

> *When Morita first came up with the idea for a portable stereo system (later called the Walkman), few people saw a market for it. In fact, Morita convinced other managers to back the project by promising to resign from his job if Sony did not sell 100,000 units within a year.*
>
> *"It embarrassed me to be so excited about a product most others thought would be a dud," he noted. "But I was so confident . . . that I said I would take personal responsibility for the project. I never had reason to regret it."*

As Morita traveled around the world, he often saw young people lugging huge portable stereo systems to the beach or to the park. He knew that people enjoyed listening to pre-recorded music at home and in their cars, and he had a strong feeling that they would also like a convenient way to do so outside of these environments. "I thought many young people might like to take good stereo sound with them," he recalled. "So I asked my staff to build a small experimental cassette player with light, comfortable headphones. That's the origin of the Walkman."

Sony engineers soon designed the portable stereo system that Morita had described. But few people saw a market for the product. In fact, Morita convinced other managers to back the project by promising to resign from his job if Sony did not sell 100,000 units within a year. "It embarrassed me to be so excited about a product most others thought would be a dud," he noted. "But I was so confident . . . that I said I would take personal responsibility for the project. I never had reason to regret it." Just as Morita predicted, the Walkman stereo cassette player turned out to be Sony's biggest hit product when it was introduced in 1979. It took competitors two years to duplicate the technology, and by that time Sony had sold an amazing 20 million units worldwide.

Around the same time, however, Sony introduced the product that became its biggest flop. The company was one of the early leaders in the race to develop a videocassette recorder (VCR) for home use. Sony's VCR, which came on the market before any competing products were available, used a format called Betamax. A short time later, several other companies introduced VCRs that used a format called VHS. The two formats used different-sized videotapes and were not compatible with each other. Many people felt that the Betamax format provided better picture quality. But the VHS format played longer, so an entire movie could fit on one tape. In addition, the VHS manufacturers were more successful in licensing popular movies for their format. As a result, consumers quickly came to prefer the VHS format over Betamax. Sony stubbornly stuck with the Betamax instead of developing its own VHS machine, and before long its VCR sales dropped to nothing.

Morita learned an important lesson from the failure of the Betamax. He realized that his competitors' ability to license hit movies for the VHS format had given them an advantage with consumers. He wanted Sony to have an edge in licensing media for the future. In 1988, Sony purchased CBS Records in order to have access to a large catalog of popular music for its compact disk (CD) players. Two years later, Sony bought two American film production companies, Columbia Pictures and TriStar Entertainment, to expand its movie holdings. All of these companies lost money when Sony first took them over, which led some industry experts to criticize Morita's strategy. But as the Internet increased the importance of digital entertainment in the 1990s, Sony's purchases began to look like a good idea.

Worldwide Spokesman for Japanese Industry

In 1989, Morita became chairman of the board of Sony Corporation. By this time, Sony had grown into the world's leading producer of consumer electronics. The company employed over 100,000 workers and was among the 50 largest companies in the world. Under Morita's leadership, Sony developed a series of revolutionary new products that eventually became must-have items for consumers around the world, including the Walkman, the Watchman personal television, the Camcorder, the Playstation, and the first high-capacity floppy disks for computers. In the process, Sony helped transform "Made in Japan" into a positive symbol of high quality, innovative products.

Throughout Sony's growth, Morita was the company's most visible spokesman and promoter. In fact, he became one of the most influential

Morita holding a Sony Walkman, 1982.

businessmen in the world. Many observers claimed that he was better-known than any Japanese politician. In some ways, he acted as a goodwill ambassador for Japanese industry. For example, he explained the Japanese style of business management in several magazine articles and in his 1987 autobiography, *Made in Japan.* He noted that Japanese companies treat their employees like members of an extended family and offered them life-time employment. He claimed that this treatment increased employees' loyalty to the company and helped them keep a long-term perspective. Morita also created controversy by criticizing the American style of management. He often claimed that American business leaders made decisions with the goal of increasing short-term profits rather than focusing on long-term strategies for success. He also criticized American companies for laying off workers during hard economic times.

Later Years

On November 30, 1993, Morita collapsed during his morning tennis game. He was rushed to a hospital, where doctors operated to remove a blood clot from his brain. The blood clot left him partially paralyzed, and he had difficulty speaking. Morita spent the next year recovering at his condo-minium in Hawaii. In late 1994 he announced that he was stepping down as chairman of the board of Sony. By this time, the Japanese economy was entering a recession and Sony's profits were decreasing. Many people worried about how the loss of Morita would affect the company.

For the next few years, Morita maintained contact with Sony executives from his base in Hawaii. His longtime partner, Masaru Ibuka, died in 1997, but Morita was too ill to travel to the funeral. He finally returned to Tokyo in mid-1999. On October 3, 1999, Akio Morita died of pneumonia in a Tokyo hospital at the age of 78.

Although he did not personally invent any of Sony's well-known products, Morita was widely regarded as a major force behind the company's success. "His contributions were innovative marketing strategies and vision for potential market opportunities," Gene N. Landrum wrote in *Profiles of Genius: 13 Creative Men Who Changed the World*. According to business consultant Paul Saffo in the *Los Angeles Times*, Morita "was the person who took electronics and made it fit into our lives . . . to make our lives a little easier, a little better, a little more fun."

According to business consultant Paul Saffo in the Los Angeles Times, Morita *"was the person who took electronics and made it fit into our lives . . . to make our lives a little easier, a little better, a little more fun."*

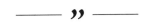

MARRIAGE AND FAMILY

Akio Morita married Yoshiko Kamei on May 13, 1950. They had two sons, Hideo and Masao, and one daughter, Naoko. At the time of Morita's death, the family had a large home in Tokyo, two country homes elsewhere in Japan, and a condominium in Hawaii. Morita's family owned nearly 10 percent of Sony's stock; their holdings had an estimated worth of $5 billion.

HOBBIES AND OTHER INTERESTS

Although Morita worked up to 12 hours per day and traveled all over the world, he still found time to enjoy a number of hobbies. He played golf for over 40 years and belonged to exclusive golf clubs in both Japan and the United States. When he was in his 50s and early 60s, he took up tennis, downhill skiing, water skiing, and scuba diving. He also earned a pilot's license and enjoyed flying his own airplanes and helicopters. Finally, Morita enjoyed listening to music throughout his life and collected antique musical instruments.

SELECTED WRITINGS

Made in Japan: Akio Morita and the Sony Corporation, 1986 (with Edwin M. Reingold and Mitsuko Shimomura)
Gakureki muyo-ron ("Never Mind School Records"), 1987
No to ieru Nippon ("A Japan That Can Say No"), 1989 (with Sintaro Ishihara)

HONORS AND AWARDS

Albert Medal (Royal Society of Arts): 1982
Order of the Legion of Honor (Government of France): 1984
First Class Order of Sacred Treasure (Emperor of Japan): 1991
Honorary Knight Commander of Most Excellent Order of the British Empire: 1992
Commander Order of Leopold (King of Belgium): 1993
Founders Medal (Institute of Electronic Engineers): 1994
Japan Society Award: 1995
Creu de Sant Jordi (Government of Spain): 1996
Distinguished Medal of Honor (Japanese American National Museum): 1996
Grand Cordon of the Order of the Rising Sun (Government of Japan): 1999
Top 20 Businessmen of the 20th Century (*Time* magazine): 1999

FURTHER READING

Books

Encyclopedia of World Biography, 1998
Hoobler, Dorothy. *Japanese Portraits,* 1994 (juvenile)
Landrum, Gene N. *Profiles of Genius: 13 Creative Men Who Changed the World,* 1993
Morita, Akio. *Made in Japan: Akio Morita and the Sony Corporation,* 1986
Nathan, John. *Sony: The Private Life,* 1999
Who's Who in the World, 1999

Periodicals

Atlantic, Nov. 1979, p.33
Current Biography 1972
Fortune, Oct. 27, 1986, p.143
Los Angeles Times, Oct. 4, 1999, p.A1

Nation's Business, Dec. 1973, p.45
New York Times, Oct. 4, 1999, p.B8
New York Times Magazine, Sep. 10, 1967, p.56
Newsweek, Dec. 13, 1993, p.50
Rolling Stone, Oct. 2, 1980, p.76
Time, Dec. 7, 1998, p.193; Aug. 23, 1999, p.104; Oct. 18, 1999, pp.21 and 41
U.S. News and World Report, July 29, 1985, p.51; Nov. 17, 1986, p.57
Washington Post, Oct. 4, 1999, p.A1

WORLD WIDE WEB SITES

http://www.sony.com
http://www.pbs.org/transistor/album1/addlbios/morita.html

Janese Swanson 1957?-
American Inventor, Entrepreneur, and Toy Designer
Founder of Girl Tech and eDames

BIRTH

Janese (pronounced ja-NEESE) Swanson was born in San Diego, California, around 1957. Her father was an air-traffic controller for the U.S. military, and her mother was a beautician. Janese was one of six children in her family.

YOUTH

Swanson first became interested in technology when she was five years old. She would sometimes accompany her father to the Marine base where he worked, and she remembers being fascinated by all the electronic gadgets in the air-traffic control center. When the United States became involved in the Vietnam War, her father was sent overseas. From this time on, her mother raised the children practically by herself.

Swanson's family was not very wealthy, but this only encouraged the young girl to be creative in her play. "We couldn't afford too many toys," her mother explained. "So she was always inventing something on her own, or trying to figure out how something worked." Throughout her childhood, Swanson took apart toasters, blenders, light switches, tape recorders, and other devices so she could figure out how they worked. Eventually, she was able to help her mother by repairing small appliances. She credits this experience with helping her to understand computers years later.

When Swanson was 10 years old, she informed her mother that she wanted to take on a newspaper route. But her mother told her that only boys were newspaper carriers. "When I was growing up, my mom couldn't help but say there were limitations to what girls do," she noted. "That was the mentality." Swanson recognized from an early age that girls received little support or encouragement to pursue non-traditional careers, particularly in the field of technology. "Unfortunately, people still reinforce the idea that boys are naturally more talented in math, computers, and science than girls," she stated.

EDUCATION

Swanson was always a good student, especially in math and science. But during her years at Orange Glen High School in Escondido, California, her teachers never pushed her to develop these skills. "I took the tests in high school that gave you the results and said here are your career choices and a little affirmation card to put in your wallet. And the areas were like, 'Be a model, be a flight attendant, be a schoolteacher and a retail salesperson,'" she recalled. "No one ever said, 'Gee Janese, you're really good at math. You should be an engineer — maybe you should think about engineering school.' And just that encouragement could have had a big effect on me."

Swanson wanted to be a doctor for many years, but she became discouraged when she learned that at that time, only a very small percentage of all medical-school graduates were women. So when she graduated from high school in 1975, she began pursuing the careers that her teachers had recommended to her. But she also continued her education, earning several degrees over the next 20 years. In 1980 she earned her bachelor's degree from San Diego State University, adding a teaching degree from the same university the following year. In 1990 she completed her master's degree in education with an emphasis in technology from the University of San Francisco.

Swanson completed her schooling in 1995 with a Ph.D. in organization and leadership from the University of San Francisco. Her dissertation, an extensive research paper that is often required to earn an advanced degree, was titled "Perceived Elements of Gender Preference in Technology Played by Elementary School Children." In it, she examined the different ways that boys and girls respond to technology. Her research confirmed her own belief that girls were being left out when it came to high-tech toys. "What I found was this glaring hole, a gap, in technology and it seemed to be growing," she noted. "What we were doing subconsciously was setting up a bias against girls. And girls were picking it up, and they were shying away from the computer as well as other technology."

> "I took the tests in high school that gave you the results and said here are your career choices and a little affirmation card to put in your wallet. And the areas were like, 'Be a model, be a flight attendant, be a schoolteacher and a retail salesperson.' No one ever said, 'Gee Janese, you're really good at math. You should be an engineer— maybe you should think about engineering school.' And just that encouragement could have had a big effect on me."

FIRST JOBS

At one time or another, Swanson worked at all of the jobs that her high-school teachers had considered appropriate for women. For example, she worked as a model for a short time and appeared on the cover of *San Diego Magazine.* "I even modeled a wetsuit once," she related. "It was very demoralizing, although I didn't wake up to that until I started doing the modeling. I was nothing but a body." She also worked in retail, selling home electronics at Sears. After earning a college degree in education, Swanson took a position as a fourth-grade teacher in Oceanside, California. She enjoyed the job, but she was laid off after a year because of budget cutbacks. At this point, she spent a brief time working as a flight attendant. "They made us wear what they called regulation lips," she remembered. "Red lipstick."

*Swanson holding the voice-activated Password Journal,
one of Girl Tech's most popular products, 1999.*

In the early 1980s, when the home-computer market was just getting started, Swanson hosted parties in her home to introduce women to software products. Her success at this job led to a position at an educational store in San Francisco, where she demonstrated computer programs for children. As she spoke with kids and their parents about software and games, she learned a great deal about what people did and did not like. For example, she discovered that girls did not like one computer game because a female cheerleader jumped up and down when they picked the right answer. She passed along this information to representatives of the software company when they stopped by the store. The company took her advice and replaced the cheerleader with a clown that would appeal to both boys and girls.

CAREER HIGHLIGHTS

Becoming an Inventor

In 1988, Swanson turned her experience selling software into a job producing computer games for Broderbund, a family-owned software maker. She became a member of the team that developed the best-selling game

"

Even though Swanson had created YakBak to appeal to both boys and girls, the company had decided to market it to boys. From this time on, she was determined to maintain control of her inventions. "I didn't realize at that time how it would be on the marketing side. We would license the toy, but all the companies in their advertising would treat girls like props and victims and cheerleaders. This is why I started the Girl Tech brand. I wanted to get control."

"

"Where in the World Is Carmen Sandiego?" This game, which led to the popular PBS TV series of the same name, teaches children geography as they track a clever female thief around the world. "It worked because it had strong content and the female character was unusual," Swanson explained of the game's success.

Although Swanson enjoyed her job at Broderbund, she did not like spending 10 hours per day at the office. By this time, she was the single mother of a young daughter, Jackie. She found that the long hours at work made it difficult to spend enough time with her daughter. One day, Swanson came up with an idea to make their time apart easier. She created a small recording device that would play back a spoken phrase at the touch of a button. Jackie could carry the device with her to day care and hear her mother say "I love you" whenever she wanted.

Creating YakBak

Before long, Swanson started to see other possibilities for her invention. She quit her job at Broderbund and started her own company, Kid One for Fun, in order to develop the device further. It eventually turned into a palm-sized electronic toy known as YakBak, which allows kids to record their voices and then play their words back at fast or slow speeds. Although Swanson's company held the exclusive rights to produce and sell her invention, she chose to license the product to a larger company called Yes Entertainment. Yes would manufacture and market YakBak, and in exchange Swanson would receive payments known as royalties.

Once Swanson agreed to license YakBak, however, she no longer controlled the way it was advertised. Yes Entertainment created a television commercial that showed a boy playing with the toy with a girl in the background. The first time Swanson and her daughter saw the commercial,

Jackie asked, "How come all the cool toys are for boys?" Even though Swanson had created the toy to appeal to both boys and girls, the company had decided to market it to boys. From this time on, Swanson was determined to maintain control of her inventions. "I didn't realize at that time how it would be on the marketing side," she explained. "We would license the toy, but all the companies in their advertising would treat girls like props and victims and cheerleaders. This is why I started the Girl Tech brand. I wanted to get control."

Founding Girl Tech

In 1995, Swanson formed a new company, Girl Tech, in order to focus on creating fun electronic toys and software products for girls. "You can build adventurous products for girls, and they don't have to be pink, they don't have to be dolls, and they don't have to be teacups for girls to like them," she explained of the company's philosophy. Girl Tech, based in San Rafael, California, started out with a small budget and five female employees. "I slapped down my credit cards and opened my home to a few believers who were willing to work for pennies to make the dream come true," Swanson recalled. "All along, there have been people committed to making the industry and the world more receptive and encouraging to girls' abilities, and not surprisingly, most are women or fathers of daughters. Though no one who showed support had much money, they had a wealth of talent, ideas, and motivation."

One of the toughest obstacles Girl Tech faced was convincing toy company executives—and many parents—that girls would be interested in technology-based toys and games. For years, many people assumed that girls simply did not like computer and video games. Industry statistics seemed to support this idea: about 85

In starting her company, Swanson says, "I slapped down my credit cards and opened my home to a few believers who were willing to work for pennies to make the dream come true. All along, there have been people committed to making the industry and the world more receptive and encouraging to girls' abilities, and not surprisingly, most are women or fathers of daughters. Though no one who showed support had much money, they had a wealth of talent, ideas, and motivation."

percent of the $10 billion worth of electronic toys sold each year were sold to boys. But Swanson found that girls were not opposed to technology at all—they just did not tend to like the sorts of electronic toys and games that were popular with boys. "They don't like the same kinds of toys boys like, but they still like electronic toys," she stated. "They need opportunities to be mischievous and adventurous, but they also really want to identify with their own gender."

The research Swanson did for her Ph.D. showed that girls do not generally like violent games and intense competition. Instead, they like playing cooperatively with other kids. They also appreciate games with female lead characters and interesting story lines. They do not like to see characters die; instead, they prefer bad guys to receive funny punishments or be turned into good guys. "When boys play at the computer, it's man against machine," Swanson explained. "Girls care about the details of the product and enjoy interaction with other girls. Because most video games are designed for boys' play patterns, girls have been left out of the technology."

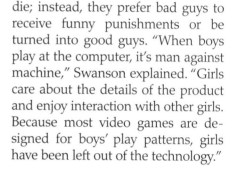

"When boys play at the computer, it's man against machine. Girls care about the details of the product and enjoy interaction with other girls. Because most video games are designed for boys' play patterns, girls have been left out of the technology."

Swanson believes that it is important for girls to be exposed to technology at an early age through toys and games. She argues that this exposure builds the computer skills girls will need later in life and opens the door to high-tech careers. "There's a real need in our culture to introduce girls to technology-based products and services at an early age. It not only increases girls' self-esteem, but helps broaden the opportunities available to them in the future," she stated. "Today is the age of the knowledge worker, and that's not going to change. If we don't offer play opportunities for girls to try on different roles of who they might become, or who they already are, to find out more about themselves and also give them an opportunity to play with technology, then they may limit their future career choices."

Introducing Girls to the Internet

One of Swanson's first priorities for Girl Tech was to find ways to introduce girls to the Internet. She started out by creating a girl-friendly web site at www.girltech. com to give girls age 6 and older a safe place to explore and

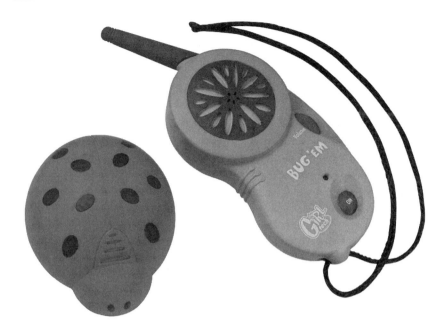

learn about the Internet. "When we typed 'girls' on our search engine, all we got was smut. All of the girls' sites were totally inappropriate," she explained. "We have developed a hip, cool, and safe place for girls to come together."

The Girl Tech web site features magazine columns, online games, and links to a variety of other girl-focused sites. It includes profiles of women who have built exciting careers in science and technology. There is also an advice columnist, Dear Auntie Em, who acts like a mentor and provides straight answers to girls' questions. Another popular feature is the Inventor's Corner, which allows girls to use their creativity to come up with ideas for new toys. The site gives girls an opportunity to connect with other girls from around the world who share an interest in technology, communication, and learning. They can even earn a merit badge in Girl Scouts for learning about interactive technology. Finally, the Girl Tech site contains resources to help parents and teachers introduce girls to technology. By 1999, the site was averaging two million hits a month from 100 countries around the world.

In 1996, Swanson's company released *Tech Girl's Internet Adventures.* In this book, a female character named Tech Girl introduces girls to various aspects of the Internet, like sending e-mail and conducting searches. "As you can see she's almost a normal girl in that she loves to skate, she loves to run, to jump, to kick, to make funny faces," Swanson said of the character. "She is not overly buxom. She is not necessarily a long-legged and large-eyed waif-looking character like what we see most often in the characters that exist out there for girls. She's actually a girl that most girls at this age level can relate to." Tech Girl also appears on the Girl Tech web site, where she helps girls explore a virtual city and learn about science.

> "There's a real need in our culture to introduce girls to technology-based products and services at an early age. It not only increases girls' self-esteem, but helps broaden the opportunities available to them in the future. Today is the age of the knowledge worker, and that's not going to change. If we don't offer play opportunities for girls to try on different roles of who they might become, or who they already are, to find out more about themselves and also give them an opportunity to play with technology, then they may limit their future career choices."

Tech Girl's Internet Adventures also includes a listing of 200 girl-oriented web sites in order to help girls travel safely through cyberspace. In addition, it comes with a CD-ROM that allows girls to design their own web pages. In 2000, Girl Tech planned to expand its Internet tools by introducing its own web browser, called Surfer Girl.

Producing Electronic Toys for Girls

In 1998, Swanson sold Girl Tech to Radica Games of Hong Kong for $6 million. She joined the Radica organization as vice president of the new girls' toy division, based around Girl Tech. Radica executives recognized that the market for electronic games aimed at boys was highly competitive. They viewed electronic products for girls as an important new opportunity. "Radica is a true learning organization with strong entrepreneurial spirit," Swanson noted. "Their top-quality innovative technologies and manufacturing give Girl Tech the necessary resources to fulfill our goal of providing fun technology to girls around the world."

Backed by Radica's resources, Girl Tech launched an entire line of personal electronic products for girls. One of the biggest successes was the Password Journal, a diary with a voice-recognition lock. It allows a girl to record a password in her own voice, and then the journal can't be opened by any

other voice. It's a great place to write secrets that brothers and sisters can't see. Password Journal became the top-selling toy in the youth electronics market for 1999. Other popular Girl Tech toys include the Beam-It slumber party projector, a type of flashlight with a transparent window. Girls can write messages on the window and then project them on the wall or ceiling, while staying up late at slumber parties. Another fun item is the Bug 'Em remote listening device, which is two separate pieces. One piece is a small bug-shaped recorder that chirps to "bug 'em," but also contains a microphone to record what people nearby are saying. The second piece is a receiver that allows girls to eavesdrop on people talking in another room. A recent addition to the Girl Tech line is the Keep Safe Box. This is a keepsake box with hidden compartments and a lock with a three-button code. The box can be opened with a remote only if you know the code.

Many of Swanson's new product ideas have been inspired by her daughter. For example, Jackie inspired the Door Pass security system, which uses voice recognition software and a password recorded by the owner. She can use it to protect her room, because it blinks to show that someone has gotten in. "Jackie used to tape 'keep out' signs all over her door," Swanson recalled. "She wanted a device to put on her door that would let her know when someone went in. We invented a voice-activated door pass, and if someone tries to go into the room without the correct password, the device says 'Access denied' and records how many times an intruder attempts to enter."

Swanson attributes her success as an inventor to "being a girl inside. I'm always a girl. I've stayed in touch with that even though I've had a lot of socialization stuff shoved down my throat about what I'm supposed to be and not supposed to be." She hopes that by introducing girls to technology, she can help the next generation of women improve their position in society. "It's up to us to validate each other, and technology is the tool," she stated. "[If] we're sending messages that girls are very valued in our society and in our world and their contributions are important no matter what they do . . . then things will be different for women."

> **"**
>
> *Swanson hopes that by introducing girls to technology, she can help the next generation of women improve their position in society. "It's up to us to validate each other, and technology is the tool . . . [If] we're sending messages that girls are very valued in our society and in our world and their contributions are important no matter what they do . . . then things will be different for women."*
>
> **"**

Current Plans

Recently, Swanson left Radica and struck off on her own again. In June 2000, she started a new company called eDames, where she is the founder and CEO (Chief Executive Officer). Like Girl Tech, eDames is dedicated to bringing technology to young women. With Swanson's reputation for combining innovative technology and fun ideas specifically for girls, her many fans are eager to see her new work with eDames!

MARRIAGE AND FAMILY

Swanson was married briefly in the mid-1980s. Her marriage produced one daughter, Jackie, before ending in divorce.

HONORS AND AWARDS

100 Best Products (Dr. Toy): 1997, for *Tech Girl's Internet Adventures*
Parent Council Award: 1997, for *Tech Girl's Internet Adventures*
Women of the Year (*Ms.* magazine): 1997

FURTHER READING

Periodicals

Arlington (Texas) Morning News, Aug. 1, 1999, p.A9
Chicago Tribune, June 29, 1997, Womanews Section, p.3
Dallas Morning News, Aug. 17, 1999, p.F2
Ms., Jan./Feb. 1997, p.37
New York Times, May 21, 1998, p.G9; Sep. 30, 1999, p.G7
Newsday, Feb. 20, 1996, p.B21
Playthings, Dec. 1998, p.68
Sacramento Bee, Jan. 23, 1996, p.A5
San Francisco Examiner, Apr. 25, 1996, p.B1; Aug. 4, 1996, p.D5; Aug. 1, 1999, p.B5

ADDRESS

87 Vista Marin Drive
San Rafael, CA 94903

WORLD WIDE WEB SITES

http://www.girltech.com
http://www.thetech.org/revolutionaries/swanson/
http://www.si.edu/lemelson/centerpieces/ilives/index.html

Photo and Illustration Credits

David Attenborough/Photos: Bill Robinson; Copyright © Hulton-Deutsch Collection/CORBIS; PBS; AP/Wide World Photos. Cover: THE LIFE OF BIRDS copyright © David Attenborough Productions, 1998. By permission Princeton University Press.

Robert Ballard/Photos: AP/Wide World Photos; JASON Foundation for Education

Benjamin Carson/Photos: Copyright © Keith Weller Photography/Johns Hopkins Children's Center; AP/Wide World Photos. Cover: GIFTED HANDS by permission of ZondervanPublishingHouse.

Eileen Collins/Photos: NASA.

Birute Galdikas/Photo: OFI; Margo Pfeiff. Cover: copyright © National Geographic Society.

Lonnie Johnson/Photos: Courtesy Johnson Research & Development Co.

Margaret Lowman/Photos: Copyright © 1996 Jan Small Photography; copyright © 1997 by Christopher G. Knight

Forrest Mars, Sr./Photos: Copyright © Neshan Naltchayan; Richard Thompson Jr.

Akio Morita/Photos: copyright © AFP/CORBIS; AP/Wide World Photos.

Janese Swanson/Photos: Thor Swift/NYT Pictures.

How to Use the Cumulative Index

Our indexes have a new look. In an effort to make our indexes easier to use, we've combined the Name and General Index into a new, cumulative General Index. This single ready-reference resource covers all the volumes in *Biography Today,* both the general series and the special subject series. The new General Index contains complete listings of all individuals who have appeared in *Biography Today* since the series began. Their names appear in bold-faced type, followed by the issue in which they appear. The General Index also includes references for the occupations, nationalities, and ethnic and minority origins of individuals profiled in *Biography Today.*

We have also made some changes to our specialty indexes, the Places of Birth Index and the Birthday Index. To consolidate and to save space, the Places of Birth Index and the Birthday Index will no longer appear in the January and April issues of the softbound subscription series. But these indexes can still be found in the September issue of the softbound subscription series, in the hardbound Annual Cumulation at the end of each year, and in each volume of the special subject series.

General Series

The General Series of *Biography Today* is denoted in the index with the month and year of the issue in which the individual appeared. Each individual also appears in the Annual Cumulation for that year.

Special Subject Series

The Special Subject Series of *Biography Today* are each denoted in the index with an abbreviated form of the series name, plus the number of the volume in which the individual appears. They are listed as follows.

Adams, Ansel . . . . Artist V.1	(Artists Series)
Cooney, Barbara . . . . Author V.8	(Author Series)
Harris, Bernard. . . . . Science V.3	(Scientists & Inventors Series)
Jeter, Derek. . . . . Sport V.4	(Sports Series)
Peterson, Roger Tory . . . . WorLdr V.1	(World Leaders Series: Environmental Leaders)
Sadat, Anwar . . . . WorLdr V.2	(World Leaders Series: Modern African Leaders)
Wolf, Hazel. . . . . WorLdr V.3	(World Leaders Series: Environmental Leaders 2)

Updates

Updated information on selected individuals appears in the Appendix at the end of the *Biography Today* Annual Cumulation. In the index, the original entry is listed first, followed by any updates.

Arafat, Yasir . . Sep 94; Update 94; Update 95; Update 96; Update 97; Update 98

Gates, Bill . . . . Apr 93; Update 98

Griffith Joyner, Florence . . . . Sport V.1; Update 98

Sanders, Barry. . . . . Sep 95; Update 99

Spock, Dr. Benjamin . . . . Sep 95; Update 98

Yeltsin, Boris . . . . Apr 92; Update 93; Update 95; Update 96; Update 98

General Index

This index includes names, occupations, nationalities, and ethnic and minority origins that pertain to individuals profiled in *Biography Today*.

167

Groening, Matt . . . . Jan 92
Gumbel, Bryant. . . . . Apr 97
Guy, Jasmine. . . . . Sep 93
Hart, Melissa Joan . . . . Jan 94
Hewitt, Jennifer Love. . . . . Sep 00
Holmes, Katie . . . . Jan 00
Hunter-Gault, Charlayne . . . . Jan 00
Jennings, Peter . . . . Jul 92
Leno, Jay . . . . Jul 92
Letterman, David. . . . . Jan 95
Lewis, Shari . . . . Jan 99
Limbaugh, Rush . . . . Sep 95
Locklear, Heather . . . . Jan 95
Madden, John . . . . Sep 97
Nye, Bill . . . . Science V.2
O'Donnell, Rosie . . . . Apr 97
Oleynik, Larisa . . . . Sep 96
Olsen, Ashley . . . . Sep 95
Olsen, Mary Kate . . . . Sep 95
Pauley, Jane. Oct 92
Perry, Luke. . . . . Jan 92
Priestley, Jason . . . . Apr 92
Roberts, Cokie. . . . . Apr 95
Sagan, Carl . . . . Science V.1
Seinfeld, Jerry . . . . Oct 92; Update 98
Shatner, William. . . . . Apr 95
Siskel, Gene. Sep 99
Smith, Will. . . . . Sep 94
Soren, Tabitha . . . . Jan 97
Stewart, Patrick . . . . Jan 94
Thiessen, Tiffani-Amber. . . . . Jan 96
Thomas, Jonathan Taylor. . . . . Apr 95
Walters, Barbara . . . . Sep 94
Wayans, Keenen Ivory . . . . Jan 93
White, Jaleel. Jan 96
Williams, Robin. . . . . Apr 92
Williamson, Kevin. . . . . Author V.6
Winfrey, Oprah. . . . . Apr 92
Zamora, Pedro . . . . Apr 95
tennis
Agassi, Andre . . . . Jul 92
Ashe, Arthur . . . . Sep 93
Evert, Chris . . . . Sport V.1
Graf, Steffi . . . . Jan 92
Hingis, Martina . . . . Sport V.2
Navratilova, Martina . . . . Jan 93; Update 94
Sampras, Pete . . . . Jan 97
Sanchez Vicario, Arantxa . . . . Sport V.1
Seles, Monica. . . . . Jan 96
Williams, Serena. . . . . Sport V.4
Williams, Venus. . . . . Jan 99

Tenzin Gyatso
see Dalai Lama . . . . Sep 98
Teresa, Mother . . . . Apr 98
Thampy, George. . . . . Sep 00
Thiessen, Tiffani-Amber . . . . Jan 96
Thomas, Clarence . . . . Jan 92
Thomas, Dave. . . . . Apr 96
Thomas, Jonathan Taylor . . . . Apr 95
Thomas, Lewis . . . . Apr 94
Tibetan
Dalai Lama . . . . Sep 98
Tompkins, Douglas . . . . WorLdr V.3
Toro, Natalia. . . . . Sep 99
track
Bailey, Donovan. . . . . Sport V.2
Devers, Gail . . . . Sport V.2
Griffith Joyner, Florence. . . . . . . Sport V.1;
Update 98
Johnson, Michael. . . . . Jan 97
Joyner-Kersee, Jackie. . . Oct 92; Update 96;
Update 97; Update 98
Lewis, Carl. . . . . Sep 96; Update 97
Rudolph, Wilma . . . . Apr 95
Travers, P.L.. . . . . Author V.2
triathalon
Smyers, Karen . . . . Sport V.4
Tubman, William V. S. . . . . WorLdr V.2
Tuttle, Merlin. . . . . Apr 97
Twain, Shania . . . . Apr 99
Uchida, Mitsuko . . . . Apr 99
Ugandan
Amin, Idi . . . . WorLdr V.2
Ukrainian
Baiul, Oksana . . . . Apr 95
United Nations
– **Ambassador to**
Albright, Madeleine . . . . Apr 97
Bush, George . . . . Jan 92
– **Secretary General**
Annan, Kofi. . . . . Jan 98
Boutros-Ghali, Boutros . . . . Apr 93;
Update 98
United States
– **Attorney General**
Reno, Janet. . . . . Sep 93; Update 98
– **First Lady**
Bush, Barbara . . . . Jan 92
Clinton, Hillary Rodham. . . . . . . Apr 93;
Update 94; Update 95; Update 96; Update 99
– **Joint Chiefs of Staff, Chairman**
Powell, Colin. . . . . Jan 92; Update 93

189

Places of Birth Index

The following index lists the places of birth for the individuals profiled in *Biography Today*. Places of birth are entered under state, province, and/or country.

195

Birthday Index

Biography Today

General Series

For ages 9 and above

Biography Today **General Series** includes a unique combination of current biographical profiles that teachers and librarians — and the readers themselves — tell us are most appealing. The **General Series** is available as a 3-issue subscription; hardcover annual cumulation; or subscription plus cumulation.

Within the **General Series**, your readers will find a variety of sketches about:

- Authors
- Cartoonists
- Musicians
- Scientists
- Political leaders
- Astronauts
- Sports figures
- TV personalities
- Movie actresses & actors
- and the movers & shakers in many other fields!

"Biography Today **will be useful in elementary and middle school libraries and in public library children's collections where there is a need for biographies of current personalities. High schools serving reluctant readers may also want to consider a subscription."*

— *Booklist,* American Library Association

"Highly recommended for the young adult audience. Readers will delight in the accessible, energetic, tell-all style; teachers, librarians, and parents will welcome the clever format, intelligent and informative text. It should prove especially useful in motivating "reluctant" readers or literate nonreaders."

— *MultiCultural Review*

"Written in a friendly, almost chatty tone, the profiles offer quick, objective information. While coverage of current figures makes *Biography Today* **a useful reference tool, an appealing format and wide scope make it a fun resource to browse."** — *School Library Journal*

"The best source for current information at a level kids can understand."

— Kelly Bryant, School Librarian, Carlton, OR

"Easy for kids to read. We love it! Don't want to be without it."

— Lynn McWhirter, School Librarian, Rockford, IL

ONE-YEAR SUBSCRIPTION
- 3 softcover issues, 6" x 9"
- Published in January, April, and September
- 1-year subscription, $56
- 150 pages per issue
- 10-12 profiles per issue
- Contact sources for additional information
- Cumulative General, Places of Birth, and Birthday Indexes

HARDBOUND ANNUAL CUMULATION
- Sturdy 6" x 9" hardbound volume
- Published in December
- $57 per volume
- 450 pages per volume
- 30-36 profiles — includes all profiles found in softcover issues for that calendar year
- Cumulative General, Places of Birth, and Birthday Indexes
- Special appendix features current updates of previous profiles

SUBSCRIPTION AND CUMULATION COMBINATION
- $99 for 3 softcover issues plus the hardbound volume

210

1992

Paula Abdul
Andre Agassi
Kirstie Alley
Terry Anderson
Roseanne Arnold
Isaac Asimov
James Baker
Charles Barkley
Larry Bird
Judy Blume
Berke Breathed
Garth Brooks
Barbara Bush
George Bush
Fidel Castro
Bill Clinton
Bill Cosby
Diana, Princess of Wales
Shannen Doherty
Elizabeth Dole
David Duke
Gloria Estefan
Mikhail Gorbachev
Steffi Graf
Wayne Gretzky
Matt Groening
Alex Haley
Hammer
Martin Handford
Stephen Hawking
Hulk Hogan
Saddam Hussein
Lee Iacocca
Bo Jackson
Mae Jemison
Peter Jennings
Steven Jobs
Pope John Paul II
Magic Johnson
Michael Jordon
Jackie Joyner-Kersee
Spike Lee
Mario Lemieux
Madeleine L'Engle
Jay Leno
Yo-Yo Ma
Nelson Mandela
Wynton Marsalis
Thurgood Marshall
Ann Martin
Barbara McClintock
Emily Arnold McCully
Antonia Novello
Sandra Day O'Connor
Rosa Parks

Jane Pauley
H. Ross Perot
Luke Perry
Scottie Pippen
Colin Powell
Jason Priestley
Queen Latifah
Yitzhak Rabin
Sally Ride
Pete Rose
Nolan Ryan
H. Norman
    Schwarzkopf
Jerry Seinfeld
Dr. Seuss
Gloria Steinem
Clarence Thomas
Chris Van Allsburg
Cynthia Voigt
Bill Watterson
Robin Williams
Oprah Winfrey
Kristi Yamaguchi
Boris Yeltsin

1993

Maya Angelou
Arthur Ashe
Avi
Kathleen Battle
Candice Bergen
Boutros Boutros-Ghali
Chris Burke
Dana Carvey
Cesar Chavez
Henry Cisneros
Hillary Rodham Clinton
Jacques Cousteau
Cindy Crawford
Macaulay Culkin
Lois Duncan
Marian Wright Edelman
Cecil Fielder
Bill Gates
Sara Gilbert
Dizzy Gillespie
Al Gore
Cathy Guisewite
Jasmine Guy
Anita Hill
Ice-T
Darci Kistler
k.d. lang
Dan Marino
Rigoberta Menchu
Walter Dean Myers

Martina Navratilova
Phyllis Reynolds Naylor
Rudolf Nureyev
Shaquille O'Neal
Janet Reno
Jerry Rice
Mary Robinson
Winona Ryder
Jerry Spinelli
Denzel Washington
Keenen Ivory Wayans
Dave Winfield

1994

Tim Allen
Marian Anderson
Mario Andretti
Ned Andrews
Yasir Arafat
Bruce Babbitt
Mayim Bialik
Bonnie Blair
Ed Bradley
John Candy
Mary Chapin Carpenter
Benjamin Chavis
Connie Chung
Beverly Cleary
Kurt Cobain
F.W. de Klerk
Rita Dove
Linda Ellerbee
Sergei Fedorov
Zlata Filipovic
Daisy Fuentes
Ruth Bader Ginsburg
Whoopi Goldberg
Tonya Harding
Melissa Joan Hart
Geoff Hooper
Whitney Houston
Dan Jansen
Nancy Kerrigan
Alexi Lalas
Charlotte Lopez
Wilma Mankiller
Shannon Miller
Toni Morrison
Richard Nixon
Greg Norman
Severo Ochoa
River Phoenix
Elizabeth Pine
Jonas Salk
Richard Scarry
Emmitt Smith

Will Smith
Steven Spielberg
Patrick Stewart
R.L. Stine
Lewis Thomas
Barbara Walters
Charlie Ward
Steve Young
Kim Zmeskal

1995

Troy Aikman
Jean-Bertrand Aristide
Oksana Baiul
Halle Berry
Benazir Bhutto
Jonathan Brandis
Warren E. Burger
Ken Burns
Candace Cameron
Jimmy Carter
Agnes de Mille
Placido Domingo
Janet Evans
Patrick Ewing
Newt Gingrich
John Goodman
Amy Grant
Jesse Jackson
James Earl Jones
Julie Krone
David Letterman
Rush Limbaugh
Heather Locklear
Reba McEntire
Joe Montana
Cosmas Ndeti
Hakeem Olajuwon
Ashley Olsen
Mary-Kate Olsen
Jennifer Parkinson
Linus Pauling
Itzhak Perlman
Cokie Roberts
Wilma Rudolph
Salt 'N' Pepa
Barry Sanders
William Shatner
Elizabeth George
    Speare
Dr. Benjamin Spock
Jonathan Taylor
    Thomas
Vicki Van Meter
Heather Whitestone
Pedro Zamora

1996

Aung San Suu Kyi
Boyz II Men
Brandy
Ron Brown
Mariah Carey
Jim Carrey
Larry Champagne III
Christo
Chelsea Clinton
Coolio
Bob Dole
David Duchovny
Debbie Fields
Chris Galeczka
Jerry Garcia
Jennie Garth
Wendy Guey
Tom Hanks
Alison Hargreaves
Sir Edmund Hillary
Judith Jamison
Barbara Jordan
Annie Leibovitz
Carl Lewis
Jim Lovell
Mickey Mantle
Lynn Margulis
Iqbal Masih
Mark Messier
Larisa Oleynik
Christopher Pike
David Robinson
Dennis Rodman
Selena
Monica Seles
Don Shula
Kerri Strug
Tiffani-Amber Thiessen
Dave Thomas
Jaleel White

1997

Madeleine Albright
Marcus Allen
Gillian Anderson
Rachel Blanchard
Zachery Ty Bryan
Adam Ezra Cohen
Claire Danes
Celine Dion
Jean Driscoll
Louis Farrakhan
Ella Fitzgerald

Harrison Ford
Bryant Gumbel
John Johnson
Michael Johnson
Maya Lin
George Lucas
John Madden
Bill Monroe
Alanis Morissette
Sam Morrison
Rosie O'Donnell
Muammar el-Qaddafi
Christopher Reeve
Pete Sampras
Pat Schroeder
Rebecca Sealfon
Tupac Shakur
Tabitha Soren
Herbert Tarvin
Merlin Tuttle
Mara Wilson

1998

Bella Abzug
Kofi Annan
Neve Campbell
Sean Combs (Puff
    Daddy)
Dalai Lama (Tenzin
    Gyatso)
Diana, Princess of Wales
Leonardo DiCaprio
Walter E. Diemer
Ruth Handler
Hanson
Livan Hernandez
Jewel
Jimmy Johnson
Tara Lipinski
Oseola McCarty
Dominique Moceanu
Alexandra Nechita
Brad Pitt
LeAnn Rimes
Emily Rosa
David Satcher
Betty Shabazz
Kordell Stewart
Shinichi Suzuki
Mother Teresa
Mike Vernon
Reggie White
Venus Williams
Kate Winslet

1999

Ben Affleck
Jennifer Aniston
Maurice Ashley
Kobe Bryant
Bessie Delany
Sadie Delany
Sharon Draper
Sarah Michelle Gellar
John Glenn
Savion Glover
Jeff Gordon
David Hampton
Lauryn Hill
King Hussein
Lynn Johnston
Shari Lewis
Oseola McCarty
Mark McGwire
Slobodan Milosevic
Natalie Portman
J. K. Rowling
Frank Sinatra
Gene Siskel
Sammy Sosa
John Stanford
Natalia Toro
Shania Twain
Mitsuko Uchida
Jesse Ventura
Venus Williams

2000

Christina Aguilera
K.A. Applegate
Lance Armstrong
Backstreet Boys
Daisy Bates
Harry Blackmun
George W. Bush
Carson Daly
Ron Dayne
Henry Louis Gates, Jr.
Doris Haddock
    (Granny D)
Jennifer Love Hewitt
Chamique Holdsclaw
Katie Holmes
Charlayne Hunter-Gault
Johanna Johnson
Craig Kielburger
John Lasseter
Peyton Manning
Ricky Martin

John McCain
Walter Payton
Freddie Prinze, Jr.
Viviana Risca
Briana Scurry
George Thampy
CeCe Winans

Biography Today

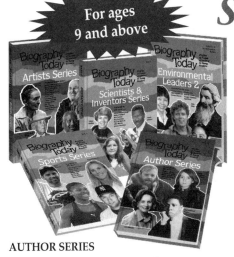

Subject Series

Expands and complements the General Series and targets specific subject areas ...

Our readers asked for it! They wanted more biographies, and the *Biography Today* **Subject Series** is our response to that demand. Now your readers can choose their special areas of interest and go on to read about their favorites in those fields. Priced at just $38 per volume, the following specific volumes are included in the *Biography Today* **Subject Series**:

- **Artists Series**
- **Author Series**
- **Scientists & Inventors Series**
- **Sports Series**
- **World Leaders Series**
  Environmental Leaders
  Modern African Leaders

FEATURES AND FORMAT

- Sturdy 6" x 9" hardbound volumes
- Individual volumes, $39 each
- 200 pages per volume
- 12 profiles per volume — targets individuals within a specific subject area
- Contact sources for additional information
- Cumulative General, Places of Birth, and Birthday Indexes

NOTE: There is *no duplication of entries* between the **General Series** of *Biography Today* and the **Subject Series**.

AUTHOR SERIES

"A useful tool for children's assignment needs." — *School Library Journal*

"The prose is workmanlike: report writers will find enough detail to begin sound investigations, and browsers are likely to find someone of interest." — *School Library Journal*

SCIENTISTS & INVENTORS SERIES

"The articles are readable, attractively laid out, and touch on important points that will suit assignment needs. Browsers will note the clear writing and interesting details." — *School Library Journal*

"The book is excellent for demonstrating that scientists are real people with widely diverse backgrounds and personal interests. The biographies are fascinating to read." — *The Science Teacher*

SPORTS SERIES

"This series should become a standard resource in libraries that serve intermediate students." — *School Library Journal*

ENVIRONMENTAL LEADERS #1

"A tremendous book that fills a gap in the biographical category of books. This is a great reference book." — *Science Scope*

Artists Series

VOLUME 1

Ansel Adams
Romare Bearden
Margaret Bourke-White
Alexander Calder
Marc Chagall
Helen Frankenthaler
Jasper Johns
Jacob Lawrence
Henry Moore
Grandma Moses
Louise Nevelson
Georgia O'Keeffe
Gordon Parks
I.M. Pei
Diego Rivera
NormanRockwell
Andy Warhol
Frank Lloyd Wright

Author Series

VOLUME 1

Eric Carle
Alice Childress
Robert Cormier
Roald Dahl
Jim Davis
John Grisham
Virginia Hamilton
James Herriot
S.E. Hinton
M.E. Kerr
Stephen King
Gary Larson
Joan Lowery Nixon
Gary Paulsen
Cynthia Rylant
Mildred D. Taylor
Kurt Vonnegut, Jr.
E.B. White
Paul Zindel

VOLUME 2

James Baldwin
Stan and Jan Berenstain
David Macaulay
Patricia MacLachlan
Scott O'Dell

Jerry Pinkney
Jack Prelutsky
Lynn Reid Banks
Faith Ringgold
J.D. Salinger
Charles Schulz
Maurice Sendak
P.L. Travers
Garth Williams

VOLUME 3

Candy Dawson Boyd
Ray Bradbury
Gwendolyn Brooks
Ralph Ellison
Louise Fitzhugh
Jean Craighead George
E.L. Konigsburg
C.S. Lewis
Fredrick McKissack
Patricia McKissack
Katherine Paterson
Anne Rice
Shel Silverstein
Laura Ingalls Wilder

VOLUME 4

Betsy Byars
Chris Carter
Caroline Cooney
Christopher Paul Curtis
Anne Frank
Robert Heinlein
Marguerite Henry
Melissa Mathison
Bill Peet
Lois Lowry
August Wilson

VOLUME 5

Sharon Creech
Michael Crichton
Karen Cushman
Tomie de Paola
Lorraine Hansberry
Karen Hesse
Brian Jacques
Gary Soto
Richard Wright
Laurence Yep

VOLUME 6

Lloyd Alexander
Paula Danziger

Nancy Farmer
Zora Neale Hurston
Shirley Jackson
Angela Johnson
Jon Krakauer
Leo Lionni
Francine Pascal
Louis Sachar
Kevin Williamson

VOLUME 7

William H. Armstrong
Patricia Reilly Giff
Langston Hughes
Stan Lee
Julius Lester
Robert Pinsky
Todd Strasser
Jacqueline Woodson
Patricia C. Wrede
Jane Yolen

VOLUME 8

Amelia Atwater-Rhodes
Barbara Cooney
Paul Laurence Dunbar
Ursula K. Le Guin
Farley Mowat
Naomi Shihab Nye
Daniel Pinkwater
Beatrix Potter
Ann Rinaldi

Scientists & Inventors Series

VOLUME 1

John Bardeen
Sylvia Earle
Dian Fossey
Jane Goodall
Bernadine Healy
Jack Horner
Mathilde Krim
Edwin Land
Louise & Mary Leakey
Rita Levi-Montalcini
J. Robert Oppenheimer
Albert Sabin
Carl Sagan
James D. Watson

VOLUME 2

Jane Brody
Seymour Cray
Paul Erdös
Walter Gilbert
Stephen Jay Gould
Shirley Ann Jackson
Raymond Kurzweil
Shannon Lucid
Margaret Mead
Garrett Morgan
Bill Nye
Eloy Rodriguez
An Wang

VOLUME 3

Luis Alvarez
Hans A. Bethe
Gro Harlem Brundtland
Mary S. Calderone
Ioana Dumitriu
Temple Grandin
John L. Gwaltney
Bernard Harris
Jerome H. Lemelson
Susan Love
Ruth Patrick
Oliver Sacks
Richie Stachowski

VOLUME 4

David Attenborough
Robert Ballard
Ben Carson
Eileen Collins
Biruté Galdikas
Lonnie Johnson
Meg Lowman
Forrest Mars Sr.
Akio Morita
Janese Swanson

Sports Series

VOLUME 1

Hank Aaron
Kareem Abdul-Jabbar
Hassiba Boulmerka
Susan Butcher
Beth Daniel
Chris Evert
Ken Griffey, Jr.
Florence Griffith Joyner
Grant Hill
Greg Lemond
Pelé
Uta Pippig
Cal Ripken, Jr.
Arantxa Sanchez Vicario
Deion Sanders
Tiger Woods

VOLUME 2

Muhammad Ali
Donovan Bailey
Gail Devers
John Elway
Brett Favre
Mia Hamm
Anfernee "Penny"
    Hardaway
Martina Hingis
Gordie Howe
Jack Nicklaus
Richard Petty
Dot Richardson
Sheryl Swoopes
Steve Yzerman

VOLUME 3

Joe Dumars
Jim Harbaugh
Dominik Hasek
Michelle Kwan
Rebecca Lobo
Greg Maddux
Fatuma Roba
Jackie Robinson
John Stockton
Picabo Street
Pat Summitt
Amy Van Dyken

VOLUME 4

Wilt Chamberlain
Brandi Chastain
Derek Jeter
Karch Kiraly
Alex Lowe
Randy Moss
Se RiPak
Dawn Riley
Karen Smyers
Kurt Warner
Serena Williams

World Leaders Series

VOLUME 1: Environmental Leaders 1

Edward Abbey
Renee Askins
David Brower
Rachel Carson
Marjory Stoneman
    Douglas
Dave Foreman
Lois Gibbs
Wangari Maathai
Chico Mendes
Russell Mittermeier
Margaret and Olaus
    Murie
Patsy Ruth Oliver
Roger Tory Peterson
Ken Saro-Wiwa
Paul Watson
Adam Werbach

VOLUME 2: Modern African Leaders

Mohammed Farah
    Aidid
Idi Amin
Hastings Kamuzu Banda
Haile Selassie
Hassan II
Kenneth Kaunda
Jomo Kenyatta
Mobutu Sese Seko
Robert Mugabe
Kwame Nkrumah
Winnie Mandela
Julius Kambarage
    Nyerere
Anwar Sadat
Jonas Savimbi
Léopold Sédar Senghor
William V. S. Tubman

VOLUME 3: Environmental Leaders 2

John Cronin
Dai Qing
Ka Hsaw Wa
Winona LaDuke
Aldo Leopold
Bernard Martin
Cynthia Moss
John Muir
Gaylord Nelson
Douglas Tompkins
Hazel Wolf